The Creation of
Imaginary
Worlds

of related interest

Unseen Worlds
Looking Through the Lens of Childhood
Kate Adams
ISBN 978 1 84905 051 7

The Spiritual Dimensions of Childhood
Kate Adams, Brendan Hyde and Richard Woolley
ISBN 978 1 84310 602 9

Dream Time with Children
Learning to Dream, Dreaming to Learn
Brenda Mallon
ISBN 978 1 84310 014 0

Listening to Children
A Practitioner's Guide
Alison McLeod
ISBN 978 1 84310 549 7

Creating Children's Art Games for Emotional Support
Vicky Barber
ISBN 978 1 84905 163 7

Creative Coping Skills for Children
Emotional Support through Arts and Crafts Activities
Bonnie Thomas
ISBN 978 1 84310 921 1

WITHDRAWN

The Creation of Imaginary Worlds

The Role of Art, Magic & Dreams in Child Development

Claire Golomb

Jessica Kingsley *Publishers*
London and Philadelphia

Extracts from Weir 1970 on pp.148–9 are reproduced
by kind permission of De Gruyter Mouton.
Extract from Nelson 1989 on p.150 is reproduced by kind permission of Elena Levy.
Extracts from Sutton-Smith 1981 on pp.152–3 are reproduced
by kind permission of Brian Sutton-Smith.

First published in 2011
by Jessica Kingsley Publishers
116 Pentonville Road
London N1 9JB, UK
and
400 Market Street, Suite 400
Philadelphia, PA 19106, USA

www.jkp.com

Library of Congress Cataloging in Publication Data
Golomb, Claire.
The creation of imaginary worlds : the role of art, magic and
dreams in child development / Claire Golomb.
p. cm.
Includes bibliographical references and index.
ISBN 978-1-84905-852-0 (alk. paper)
1. Imagination in children. 2. Child psychology. 3. Child development. I. Title.
BF723.I5.G65 2011
155.4'133--dc22

2010036636

British Library Cataloguing in Publication Data
A CIP catalogue record for this book is available from the British Library

ISBN 978 1 84905 852 0

Printed and bound in the United States by
‾‾ ‾‾‾ ‾‾‾‾‾ , Inc.

In memory of
Maya

Acknowledgments

I thank the following individuals and institutions for permission to reproduce selected monologues and stories: Brian Sutton-Smith for selections from *The Folk Stories of Children*, Elena Levy and Harvard University Press for a monologue from *Narratives from the Crib*, and The Gruyter Mouton for monologues from Ruth Hirsch Weir's *Language in the Crib*. Special thanks to Mali Golomb-Leavitt for her expert assistance with some of the illustrations. Finally, I want to express my deep appreciation to Lisa Clark, my editor, for her generous support.

Contents

List of Plates

List of Figures

Preface

The early childhood years are, perhaps, the most remarkable period in human development during which a predominantly sensory-motor infant becomes a symbol-creating human being. Every day brings new discoveries and challenges for the infant, the toddler, and the young preschooler: how to deal with the strangers he or she meets, objects seen for the first time that ask to be held, squeezed, squished, tasted, named, and explored in numerous other ways. The challenges and joys of walking, running, climbing, riding a tricycle, then bicycle, throwing and catching a ball and, of course, using language to convey one's wishes and, whenever possible, to command the world. In a relatively short period of time, the toddler acquires a good deal of knowledge about everyday objects, about cause and effect, about such concepts as before and after, here and there, about his or her desires ("I want...") and the intentions of others. We marvel at the speed with which so much knowledge about the real world is acquired and incorporated into the preschool child's mind.

At the same time that the preschooler's attention seems wholly focused on the outer world and how it is to be understood and managed, another domain emerges that engages the child's imagination and with it the power to transform reality, often in emotionally heightened tones. This marks the spontaneous appearance of make-believe actions, of pretense play and the discovery of forms on paper, all creative inventions that enrich and empower the childhood years and well beyond.

To gain a more intimate understanding of how emotionally significant this world of the imagination can be, I recently viewed a large collection of drawings, poems, stories, birthday wishes, weavings, collages, and other artworks that cover the childhood period, from approximately age 3 years to 11–12. There is much that can be said about this collection, about developmental changes in form, color use, style, content, medium, originality, etc., but the most striking findings for me were the deeply felt emotions of the child artist and poet who used the various media to express her feelings about the different family members, especially the parent, creating a record of the passions, joys, regrets, and worries that characterize much of the inner lives and loves of children. This rich record of important events in a child's life, of birthdays, holidays, changing seasons, struggles, conflicts, and achievements provides a glimpse into a part of the child's mental and emotional life that is not always visible to the parent, and even if acknowledged is probably not fully understood or valued. It is for this reason that I am writing this book for parents, teachers, and students of early child development who wish to gain a better understanding of child art, make-believe play, imaginary playmates, dreams and stories, all aspects of the mental ability to create imaginary worlds, one of the mainsprings of human creativity, often a source of comfort and healing.

I shall begin my account with child art, the creation of forms on paper, with clay, or collages of cut-outs. Each one of these projects calls for complex mental and perceptual-motor actions on materials that, magically, yield recognizable shapes. The forms and figures created in this process are not just cognitive products of an adventurous mind, they are infused with emotion and linked to the child's active fantasy life. Although there are no sharp dividing lines between the diverse domains of the imagination, for clarity's sake I shall describe developments in child art, pretense play, dreams, fantasy and fiction in separate chapters.

1

The Evolution
of Child Art

Children's drawings and paintings tend to decorate the refrigerator in the kitchen and, occasionally, invade the family room as well. Many a youngster has wondered why their art is not admired throughout the house, and parents too have puzzled over the status of their child's work. Is it art? Is it play? Should it be taken seriously and gain greater prominence in the family home? We shall begin the story of children's fascination with art making during their second or third year when they first come in contact with art materials and gradually discover what can be done with them. Next, we shall outline the developmental patterns that emerge quite spontaneously, that typically characterize all early beginnings and are easily recognized across time and space. Going beyond a description of general developmental trends, we shall consider the motivation that sustains young children's interest for years to come while highlighting individual differences and the role that talent and education play in the evolution of child art.

We take as our starting point toddlers, who from an early age show an interest in the marks their actions produce. Wielding crayons, markers or pencils they quickly note that their movements leave an imprint on paper or any other surface that is within easy reach. Their gestures are shaped by the mechanical structure of the arm, the wrist, and the hand which favor curved paths and yield the early scribbles. With a hand that grips a brush or marker, toddlers soon develop a repertoire of actions that produce distinct graphic marks: forward and return motions, that is, a movement toward and away from the body, stabbing motions, and soon thereafter a rotational action that yields whirls of various densities. Depending on the availability of such material as brushes and paint, markers or crayons, 2- and 3-year-olds may pay some attention to the boundary of the paper surface, explore the visual effects they have created, and show a momentary delight in the result (see Figure 1a). Although clearly interested in the physical action and its visual effects, they do not claim ownership of their work which appears somewhat later when the first recognizable shapes emerge that capture the child's attention in novel ways. Making a stable and recognizable form marks a genuine achievement for the preschooler who has gained control over the earlier continuous rotational movement. It is not an easy feat to inhibit the urge to continue the familiar scribble motion, that is, to lift the marker and intentionally change its direction which creates a bounded closed shape, a circular form. It is this form that makes the primal distinction between what lies inside and outside its boundary, a very first step of creating pictorial space (see Figure 1b).

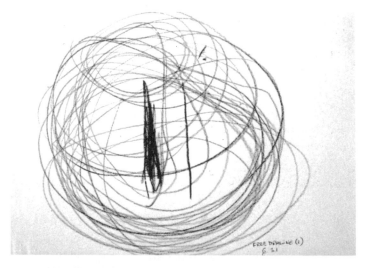

Figure 1a *Scribble Whirl. Girl, 3 years 11 months*

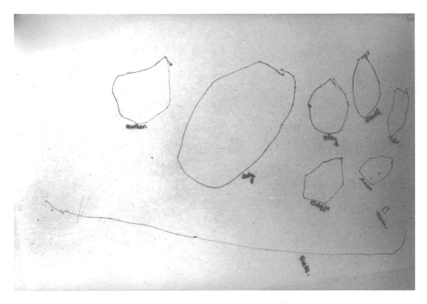

Figure 1b *First Representations: The circular shape can stand for almost any object. Boy, 3 years 4 months*

With this newly-won competence to create shapes, representational development takes off and recognizable forms and figures emerge. A recognizable form such as a drawn circle or oval resembles a real object, for example, a ball, moon, or a cookie; it can represent or symbolize an absent entity which is a true milestone in the child's cognitive and artistic development. A drawn form can now carry meaning independent of the action that produced it, and with some markings placed inside the bounded shape it quickly becomes a human or an animal, most commonly a human. Unlike the earlier scribble motions, drawing becomes an intentional act that imparts a sense of ownership over the product the child has created. Along with the ability to create forms and figures comes a desire to make colorful designs.

While age norms are not very meaningful at this stage of development, and individual variations are quite striking, between the ages of 3 and 4 years most children invent a basic human figure which signifies the beginning of the development of child art. A whole new world opens up as the child's repertoire of forms and figures begins to expand and a new relationship is forged between the artist and the creations over which he or she can rule. To exercise control over the fate of one's subjects can be exhilarating and also scary as the young artist discovers the power to create and to eliminate, to embellish and to destroy.

Representational art and early models

The early human and animal figures are *Globals*, composed of a basic circular form and facial features that identify it as an animate figure. The circular shape denotes the quality of *thingness*, by which I mean that it stands for the general quality of a solid and tangible object. The global humans and animals are not the offspring of a ready-made graphic model or photograph, they are very different from picture book illustrations and are not meant to be copies of real people or animals. These global figures represent the child's discovery or, more precisely, invention of a drawing system in which simple forms stand for the vastly more complex three-dimensional object. This ability to capture resemblance in an abstract manner speaks of a uniquely human capacity and marks the beginning of representational development in this domain. It is important to stress that the child does not mistake his or her creation for the real thing but is evolving a graphic logic that states that a simple unit, such as an oblong with facial features, can stand for another more complex unit, in this case a human or an animal. Inventing this conception of graphic equivalence is a true indicator of intelligence; it underlies all artistic development in childhood and beyond. These graphic inventions are a uniquely human achievement, beyond the capacity of even our closest primate relatives, the chimpanzees, who are able to recognize photographs, take pleasure at wielding a brush and paints, and though they can be trained to communicate with signs do not create the basic global representations most 3-year-old children produce quite spontaneously (see Figures 2a–c). This ability to "represent" is a remarkable gift; it implies that the young artist can adopt a dual approach to the paper surface and its markings, dealing with the paper as a physical substance useful for making marks, but these marks are not merely blobs of paint, they point beyond themselves to a mental reality, a domain of the imagination.

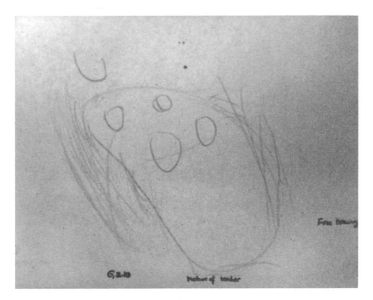

Figure 2 *Global Human*
Figure 2a *Girl, 2 years 10 months*

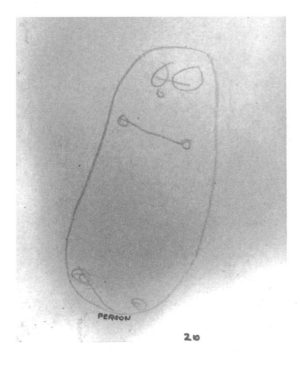

Figure 2b *Boy, 2 years 10 months*

Figure 2c *Girl, 3 years 3 months. Boy, 3 years 8 months*

Of course, children are not concerned with the formulation of rules; their interest is captured by the discoveries they make—creating a recognizable figure where there was nothing before can be an exhilarating event. Indeed, the invention of the global figure presents a step in the long process of creating a pictorial world, but it is limited in the power to convey meaning and soon gives way to a somewhat more differentiated figure composed of a separately drawn circle and limbs, the *tadpole figure*. Most adults, quite spontaneously, recognize this figure as representing a person but they are puzzled by the sparse and peculiar design that features a big head and legs. "Why is the body missing?" is a frequently heard complaint. But the body is not really absent in these drawings; it is subsumed in the large circle or, alternatively, implied between the two vertical lines that represent the legs which also serve as the body's contour. One can easily verify the existence of the body or torso by asking a simple question: "Does it have a tummy?" and if so, "Can you show me where?" From the child's point of view, the drawn figure is not incomplete, and not all one knows needs to be depicted which is, of course, true for adult artists as well. Although the generic tadpole figure can depict a person or an animal, the latter is often further specified by the addition of ears and a tail (see Figures 3a–d).

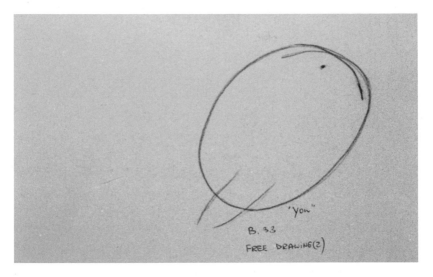

Figure 3 *Tadpole Figures: The Global Human sprouts legs, arms hair, and ears*
Figure 3a *Boy, 3 years 3 months*

Figure 3b *Boys, 3 years 6 months and 4 years 7 months*

Figure 3c *Girl, 3 years 9 months. Boy, age 4*

Figure 3d *Tadpole cat. Boy, 4 years 2 months. The young artist intended to draw a cat, but upon inspection of the figure (left), he renamed it a "cat-boy." He endowed the next figure (right) with four legs, a tail, ears, and fuzzy hair to distinguish it from its human counterpart*

The tadpole drawings of early graphic development are found universally; they appear across cultures and different time periods in the drawings of children and adults, and also make an appearance in the work of such modern artists as Paul Klee. Despite its common structure, no tadpole is quite like another and the individual style of the drawer emerges quite distinctly in the form, size, and selection of features, characteristics that often can be recognized over weeks and even months. While economy of form seems to be an early rule for the beginner who struggles to create the basic units, there is individuality, charm, and sometimes humor in the choice of elements, for example, inclusion of pupils, eyebrows, eyelashes, nostrils, tongue, hair, and ears. Drawings are often accompanied by an extensive narrative, a conversation with the figure that emerges on the page, commenting on omissions and criticizing its shortcomings: "he is not going to have..."; "it needs feet but I won't make them..."; "he [dad] is too lazy to put his tie on..."; "I'll make a person with no eyes..."; "he broke his leg, comes from the hospital..." Conversations between the child artist and her creation are not the only forms of criticism that the youngster faces; witness the following exchange between two sisters, the younger of whom draws mostly armless people and frequently omits a trunk: A (4 years 6 months): "You made his hair too long and you forgot the stomach..." M (6 years): "Silly, you can't see the stomach under the dress." A: "Your people are funny; they touch the sky with their head." As these comments indicate, the simple structure of the early drawings does not signify a lack of knowledge but ought to be seen as a phase in acquiring graphic differentiation.

In these early drawings, much is left out because it is too difficult and not essential for the basic structure of the human which can be elaborated verbally. From the ongoing commentary we note that the child does not feel compelled to represent all he or she knows. There is room for playfulness in such comments as "his head is chopped off," "his head is floating away," "looks like an octopus," "a silly man, a clown." The verbal interpretation which clarifies and also completes the drawing can be quite sophisticated, with a reference to invisible parts, as in the case of Michael, a young preschooler (age 3 years) who decides to draw a rabbit. He begins with the eyes and lists the parts one by one: eyes, nose, mouth, whiskers, ears, legs, head. His final act consists of a large circle that encloses the whole figure and he proclaims that it is the body of the rabbit and "you can't see the tail because his body is so fat."

An awareness that the simple tadpole figure is but a minimal representation and the eagerness to experiment and improve on this simple model is nicely demonstrated by Heather (age 3 years 4 months) who, having drawn her mommy and feeling dissatisfied with the result, asked her visitor to draw a person. The visitor complied and as Heather watched closely she asked about every part as it was drawn. When the mouth was outlined she asked: "those are the lips?" Following the completion of the drawing, Heather got her own paper and, while drawing, reported that she was making the eyes, nose, and mouth; the latter appears for the first time in her drawing. Touching her own lips she stated: "I am drawing two lips" and proceeded to draw three parallel lines, the middle one for the mouth, the others for the two lips.

The urge to tell a story, to depict the important people and events in the child's life, to embellish the picture, to play with forms and colors all lead to further experimentation and graphic differentiation. This is nicely illustrated in drawings that first increase the length of the tadpole figure and extend its legs, followed by the addition of a bellybutton, and somewhat later by a horizontal line to indicate where the tummy ends (see Figures 4 and 5a–c).

Figure 4 *Open Trunk Figures. Girls, 3 years 4 months and 3 years 9 months*

Figure 5 *Humans with Clearly Marked Torso*
Figure 5a *Boy, 4 years 6 months*   Figure 5b *Girl, 5 years 2 months*

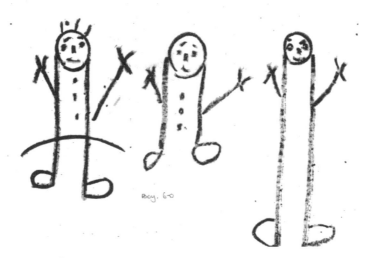

Figure 5c *Boy, age 6*

Within a relatively short time humans tend to boast a separately formed trunk, clothing, and hairstyle to suggest gender, and size differences to indicate the age of the protagonists (see Figures 6a–e). Despite these new accomplishments, there remains a significant gap between the child's intention to capture the individual characteristics of the person, in this case the mother, and the emerging figure: "My mommy has a wriggly face—it is hard to make—and long hair... [as she draws]...my mommy, her eyes are funny, her hair is in her mouth...I forgot the knees, but that's all right...that's for her legs; I can't make them straight...I can make the head too, and the hair. I'll make a picture of her wearing earrings and a necklace. But I can't make them beautiful...now—a neck so I can put a necklace on it" (girl, 4 years 4 months).

Figure 6 *Graphic Differentiation of the Human Figure. Ages range from 4 years 3 months to 7 years 4 months*
Figure 6a

Figure 6b

Figure 6c

Figure 6d

Figure 6e

I have emphasized the drawings of humans which hold a special place in children's lives, but of course, animals too are favorite subjects. After an early tadpole drawing phase, animals can be distinguished from humans by their horizontally drawn body that is endowed with some of the defining marks of the species, for example, spots and a long neck on a giraffe, udders and a bell on a cow, a profile head and floppy ears on a dog, and whiskers on a cat (see Figures 7a–e). Humans and animals are, of course, not the only objects of interest to children and the process of graphic differentiation described so far represents a more general trend that can be seen in the depiction of such diverse objects as houses, cars, airplanes, spacemen, flowers, and trees that capture the child's interest. The developmental progression outlined so far occurs, approximately, between the ages of 5 and 7 years.

Figure 7 *Animal Drawings. The Development of Graphic Differentiation*
Figure 7a *Global representation of a kitten and giraffe. The kitten is depicted as a rounded mass of fluffy fur with prominent eyes. The giraffe is identified by its vertical extension. Boy, 3 years 11 months*

Figure 7b *Age of artists, 5 years 6 months and 6 years 2 months*

Figure 7c *Artist age 5 years 5 months*

Figure 7d *Artist age 6 years 4 months*

Figure 7e *Artist age 5 years 4 months*

Familiarity with the medium and repeated practice have yielded proficiency in the drawing of lines and basic geometric shapes that are now made easily and quickly and thus facilitate the construction of more numerous items. Having mastered the basic forms, the child is no longer struggling with control over the pencil and marker, and the pleasure in creating multiple items is quite evident. Although, the human figure is still composed of simple shapes, of ovals, rectangles, and triangles, and most commonly drawn in frontal view, the drawings display greater attention to detail, to size differences, and better body proportions (see Figures 8a–b), all of which point to an ongoing process of problem solving. In the words of this 4-year-old: "I found a new way for toes and fingers…I thought and I thought and I just thinked it up."

Figure 8 *Progressive Differentiation of Size and Proportion*
Figure 8a *Girl, 6 years 6 months*

Figure 8b *Girl, 9 years 3 months*

In constructing the human figure, the body parts are made one at a time, carefully attached to provide continuity, with single lines representing the limbs (see Figures 6a–c). This kind of procedure yields a generic prototype of the human figure, which is a real accomplishment, but soon the desire to create a better likeness leads to further refinements in the ability to depict a person. Figures now tend to be drawn with a sweeping outline that fuses the major body parts into a unified whole, and the earlier one-dimensional limbs are replaced by two-dimensional contours. Drawing a continuous outline that encompasses the diverse body parts requires a greater degree of planning than the earlier drawing of separately delineated body parts that follow a top-to-bottom sequence (see Figures 9a–c).

Figure 9 *Gender Related Characteristics of Figures Drawn with a Continuous Outline*
Figure 9a *Girl, age 6*

Figure 9b *Children, ages 6 years 2 months to 6 years 9 months*

Figure 9c *Boy, age 8*

A new and more integrated conception of the drawing process and its visual effects seems to underlie this strategy that also begins to address the problem of the so-called "transparencies." This term refers to drawings of body parts that, though not visible from the viewer's station point, are represented by lines that might best be eliminated. Such is the case when previously drawn parts are overlaid with later ones, for example, when the body of a person is first outlined and then outfitted with clothing. Other forms of transparency are more deliberate in nature; they represent the child's attempt to tell the *whole* story and include such important details as a pregnant mommy drawn with a baby in her womb, or a house depicted with its outside as well as its interior made visible. In these cases, the picture is meant to represent information deemed essential and the contour of body and house stands for the inside as well as the outside of the object (see Figures 10a–b).

Figure 10 *Transparencies: Depiction in the same space of the inside and outside of an object*
Figure 10a *A baby in its mother's womb. Girl, 4 years 4 months*

Figure 10b *The birthday party represents both an external and internal view of house and party. Girl, age 12*

Along with changes in the formal characteristics of the drawings and the mastery of basic representational shapes, color begins to play a more prominent role. Drawings now tend to be richly colored and embellished with decorative designs that yield the expressive compositions so typical of the child art style. This style will dominate the early and middle childhood years, it is predominantly two-dimensional in character with as yet little interest in simulating three-dimensional space. The beauty of child art lies in this combination of form and color that has inspired many artists, especially the artists who revolutionized modern art (see Plates 1a and b on p.65).

Child art blossoms

With the facility to produce some of the basic shapes, children can use their drawings to serve multiple functions, and art making becomes more prominent in their daily activities. Drawing and painting are engaged in for entertainment, as a fun activity, as a gift to the child's loved ones, to record special events such as holidays, birthdays, sports, unusual events such as earthquakes and comets, but they also serve as an emotional outlet for intense desires, fears, worries, struggles, and conflicts. With their enriched repertoire of forms, brilliant and contrasting colors, and extensive ornamentation, the drawings and paintings convey many of the childhood interests and concerns.

As their ambition to portray events increases, children come face to face with the many constraints of the two-dimensional paper. Quite early on, a preschooler may face the question of how to represent the front and the back side of an object, for example, a cat sitting on its tail or a rabbit with a fat bottom. Some fleeting efforts may include turning the paper to the other side, but of course, this does not lead to a graphically satisfying solution and reinforces a tendency to concentrate on the frontal part of the object and to complete the story verbally. Indeed the dominant tendency is to portray all figures in a view that indicates who the people are and what they look like, and it is the frontal view that can provide relevant information about age and gender, with clothing and hairdo aiding in the distinction between males and females, the young and the old. This orientation is also useful for the elaboration of such individual characteristics as eyeglasses, earrings, jewelry, braids, hair-bands, braces, missing teeth, mustache, belts, ties, brand names on clothing, and other signs that aid in the identification of the figures. The much preferred frontal view, however, is limited in the power to portray such actions as running, chasing, kicking, lifting, reaching, bending, hugging, and many other activities. The desire to convey action propels the young artists to experiment with deviations from the frontal view as they explore ways to depict a person in different poses.

New pictorial problems arise when the child, drawing a side view of a person, discovers that some parts are no longer visible from the chosen point of view, and thus the lines that depict these invisible body parts ought to be deleted. In the case of the human face which is defined by its symmetry, most prominently the two eyes, a profile drawing calls for the omission of one eye which conflicts with the desire to depict the whole person. Gradually, a new approach to drawing takes shape and a closer inspection of the object begins to guide the child's attempt to draw a more naturalistic looking outline as in the drawing of 7-year-old Micah who makes a portrait of his grandmother. She is seated at the kitchen table, at right angles to him, and as he studies her intensively he looks back and forth between the sitter and his lines, makes corrections, includes glasses, jewelry, and clothing, and struggles with the difficulty to create a likeness in three-quarter view. Of course, the drawing falls short of his intention and he is displeased with the outcome.

As I have pointed out previously, there are good reasons for the child's allegiance to frontality in drawing since it is the frontal view of the person that provides the most detailed information about the individual's age, gender, mood, and intentions. It is during the middle childhood years that the desire to portray action and more complex social relations provokes an artistic conflict that pits the somewhat static completeness of the frontal orientation against a more dynamic vision that highlights some aspects at the cost of deleting others. Depending on the demands of the theme, children now make efforts to go beyond the singular frontal aspect to depict rear and side views of the actors. When such views also include the elimination of lines that are not visible from the drawer's perspective, the figure gains in vitality and depth as in the case of a mother who carries her baby in her arms, a person depicted in side or, infrequently, in three-quarter view. Indeed, the more precocious and talented drawers tend to experiment with the rotation of figures and also foreshortening, a technique for indicating the solidity or depth of a figure by proportionately contracting some of its parts (see Figures 11a–e). However, for the majority of children the frontal view of the human figure remains the preferred mode of representation.

Figure 11 *Beyond Simple Frontality*
Figure 11a *Mother and baby; successful elimination of lines that are hidden from view. Girl, 5 years 10 months*

Figure 11b *Movement and gestures; the dynamics of a side view. Girl, age 7*

Figure 11c *Figure depicted in three-quarter view. Boy, age 16*

Figure 11d *Foreshortened view of a seated child. Girl, age 10*

Figure 11e *Rotation and foreshortened view. Boy, age 13*

The desire to go beyond the limitation inherent in a single frontal view is not limited to the human figure. Houses now tend to be portrayed with more than the standard frontal view, with sides that are drawn as an extension of the frontal view and that maintain the overall right-angular relations (see Figures 12a–b). Some time thereafter, a distinction may be introduced between the front and the side view by using a slanting-diagonal line that recedes from the frontal plane and suggests the depth dimension of the object. A similar transformation can be observed in the drawing of such objects as boxes, cubes, tables, and other man-made objects. Going beyond the depiction of a single face of the object, for example in drawing a table, children first discover the use of adding vertically and horizontally parallel lines to display an additional side, and then move to parallel oblique lines that are very good at representing the solidity and extension of an object (see Figures 12c–d; see also Figure 10b for another depiction of a tabletop and the birthday cake).[1]

Figure 12 *Drawings of House and Table*
Figure 12a–b *The frontal view of the house is extended by appending one or two side views to its horizontal axis. Ages 8–10*

Figure 12b

Figure 12c *The table top is extended vertically by a set of parallel lines. Girl, 12 years 11 months*

Figure 12d *The sides of the table top are presented by parallel oblique lines that create a realistic looking table. Boy, 12 years 3 months*

Of course, children do not limit themselves to the depiction of single objects and we now turn to the manner in which they create on the flat two-dimensional medium of paper a pictorial space that includes multiple items.

The organization of pictorial space

The problem of how to represent the solidity of objects that take up different positions in space is of course a formidable task for the artist who confronts the two-dimensional medium of drawing. As their ambition to portray events increases, children come face to face with the many constraints of the two-dimensional paper. In order to organize multiple figures on the paper space the location and orientation of items vis-à-vis each other has to be specified: this involves relations of side-by-side, above or below, near or far. The earliest rule invented by the drawing child consists of ordering the items on the horizontal axis, side-by-side, suggesting left–right relations. Next comes the fundamental distinction between what is up and what is down, the distinction between the ground below and the sky above, and the vertical axis of the paper serves this function.

Children tend to use the bottom of the page to indicate the ground, and reserve the top for the sun, clouds, or birds which illustrates the progress they have made in the differentiation of pictorial space (see Figures 13a–d). New problems, however, arise with the vertical up–down axis which also serves to represent the near–far relation as in the drawing of a game of hopscotch where the players overlap with the clouds in the sky. Unwittingly, a perplexing situation has been created which the drawer did not anticipate (see Figure 13e).

Figure 13 *Early Rules for Organizing Pictorial Space*
Figure 13a–d *Items are drawn side-by-side along a horizontal axis, on a stand line, or aligned with the bottom of the page. Further distinctions are made between up and down, between the ground and the sky by depicting a sun, moon, clouds, birds, or stars. Ages 6–9*

Figure 13b

Figure 13c

Figure 13d

Figure 13e *Hopscotch. The vertical axis serves the dual function of representing both depth and height with the result that the hopscotch pattern overlaps with clouds and sky. Age 9*

How do children deal with the problem of depicting depth and distance, with in front-behind relations? Presented with a scene in which a series of items are placed one behind the other, and asked to reproduce them in drawing, children at first tend to draw them side by side, with the closer item drawn first, and the farther item drawn second. From this observation we can learn that they are using an ordering rule, but one that does not distinguish between left–right and near–far directions. Upon inquiry, it is apparent that the children see the objects in their proper orientation in space, they see that the two items are overlapping when looked at from a fixed station point, but they don't find an adequate pictorial solution. The logic that guides their drawing is based on a desire to depict the complete object, a rule not to be violated lightly. Somewhat later, usually during the middle childhood years, between the ages of 8 and 10 years, the challenge to depict spatial relations more accurately leads children to partially occlude the far object by the near one, an important discovery for representing the missing third dimension. When a theme is very compelling, such as drawing two children playing a hide-and-seek game, even 6-year-olds spontaneously invent techniques of partial occlusion, for example, drawing only the head of the child peeping out from behind a tree (see Figure 14).

Figure 14 *The Depiction of Spatial Relations and the Coordination of Constituent Parts. Partial occlusion of the figure in a game of hide and seek. Artist is a first grader, age 6*

Time and again we find that the drawing child has a great deal more knowledge than what he or she can display in a drawing, and that the acquisition of pictorial skills depends on such factors as the age of the child, the nature of the theme, motivation and practice, talent and training, and to some extent on the models prevailing in the culture.

Having discovered the problem inherent in using the same vertical axis for both height and depth, children invent various intermediate solutions, for example, increasing the size of the paper to accommodate multiple items, reducing the size of a figure and moving it up on the page, using partial overlap of items and eliminating invisible lines, introducing color gradients that connect foreground, middle ground and background, or the application of a lightly colored background that suggests the illusion of an expanding space.

By the middle of the childhood years (7 or 8 to 11) most children discover some of the techniques that suggest volume and depth. Over the years they have acquired a great deal of experience with the medium by observing their peers, studying models, experimenting with different techniques until they find a satisfying way to depict the themes that are dear to them. Of course, they may also have had the benefit of teacher instruction. On their own, very few children discover size diminution with distance, shading, cross-hatching, texture gradients, linear and aerial perspective, to mention some of the prominent pictorial depth cues which, if at all acquired, are a function of training. Highly motivated and talented children may well teach themselves some of these techniques, mostly by studying available models and, in the case of perspective, deducing the principles that underlie one-point linear perspective whose lines converge on a vanishing point. However, linear perspective, an invention of the artists of the Renaissance, is beyond the scope of child art and only a few adolescents seem to become familiar with this technique.

Composition as visual thinking

Drawings are meant to tell a story or to express feelings but, unlike the orally told story, the paper or canvas can capture only one moment in time and space. In telling a story, we tend to refer to the past, report on the present, and hint at future developments. Limited to a single frame in drawing, and using the pictorial tools of line, form, space, and color, how do children compose a picture to convey their message? As we have seen so far, children do not discover the possibilities and the constraints of the medium overnight, and it is in the act of drawing and painting that they confront unanticipated challenges that call for new, more satisfying pictorial strategies.

To tell a story in a drawing requires forethought and planning of the composition and, above all, the adoption of effective grouping strategies that can depict the theme. When we study children's drawings we find that they use two basic forms of compositional strategies: a gridlike alignment of figures along the horizontal and vertical axes of the paper and a centering strategy that organizes items around a pictorial center.

In the early compositions, the focus is on the number and type of items that convey the story line and little attention is paid to the arrangement of the figures. In an early and very short-lived phase, 3-year-olds tend to distribute forms in a seemingly random fashion across the page, which is followed by a tendency to cluster objects without regard for their orientation. Establishing proximity through clustering of the drawn items is an early and primitive form of depicting a relationship, as if to say: these items belong together (see Figure 15a). Soon thereafter, preschoolers begin to organize their figures along one or more horizontal axes; they thus introduce directionality into the picture by aligning the figures one by one on an imaginary stand-line. At first, these alignments are imprecise and create the impression of objects floating in space, but gradually these alignments become more organized, with attention to the size of the figures and the distance between them. This more orderly alignment is quite adequate when the intention is to make a portrait of the family, not unlike a photographer lining up all the members before clicking the camera. All the actors are portrayed in frontal view; the line-up may even signify the particular standing in the family hierarchy, for example, with the children arranged according to their age (identified by a numeral or name) or, alternatively, the children flank the parents on either side of their central position with, at times, a suggestion of favoritism that singles a child out as close to the parent (see Figures 15b–d).

Figure 15 *Family Relations*
Figure 15a *Proximity of elements through clustering. Girl, 5 years 7 months*

Figure 15b *Side-by-side alignment of the family members. Girl, 4 years 8 months*

Figure 15c *Alignment of family members according to size and/or age, with the youngest depicted as a tadpole. Boy, 5 years 8 months*

Figure 15d *Grouping of family members: children in the middle and the parents as bookends. Boy, age 8*

Going beyond an alignment on an imaginary horizontal axis, we next note the introduction of a ground or base line that anchors all the figures in the common plane. Although this configuration is better organized and clearly recognizable, simple alignments of same-size figures are constrained in the information they can convey and we see among the somewhat older children, the 5- and 6-year-olds, some efforts to group figures to indicate a relationship or a common interest. Examples can be found in the many family drawings in which the parents stand side-by-side, drawn larger than the children who are grouped according to their ages and declining size. Another example can be seen in drawings of a classroom: the teacher is drawn prominently and in some detail, distinguished by her large size, seated at some distance from the children who are grouped together, drawn in a near identical format, often with minimal differentiation that contrasts with the carefully drawn teacher. Of course, such a depiction tells us a great deal about the power relations in the classroom, the hierarchical relations that obtain between teacher and students, and the dependency and lack of distinction of her charges (see Figures 16a–c).

Figure 16a–c *Teacher Reading a Story. The teacher, large in size, looms over her tiny charges portrayed as Globals or miniscule stick figures. Ages 6–8*
Figure 16a

Figure 16b

Figure 16c

Grouping principles are powerful tools in conveying a message in the highly condensed format of a single frame, and it is during the middle childhood years that children begin to employ groupings by size, figural differentiation, location, distance, color, and type of activity. Depending on the theme, sub-groupings indicate that the items belong together or that the actors have a special relationship or a common interest as seen in drawings of birthday parties, playing ball, a picnic, picking apples in an orchard and others (see Figures 17a–e). This ability to group the items requires enhanced planning skills and, along with the growing competence to create more differentiated and recognizable figures, it is the enhanced organization of the elements that yields more meaningful statements. Although the compositions are still based on the horizontal and vertical grid, they have gained in aesthetic appeal as well as the power to communicate. Of course, a major element in the attraction these paintings hold for the child artist as well as the adult observer lies in the dramatic use of color.

Figure 17 *Grouping of Elements by Theme, Mood, or Activity. Age of artists 7–11*
Figure 17a

Figure 17b

Figure 17c

Figure 17d

Figure 17e

The second compositional strategy, mentioned before, can be seen in the tendency to center figures on a page and to create symmetrical arrangements. To use a dictionary definition, symmetry can be defined as the correspondence in size, shape, and relative position of items that are drawn on opposite sides of a dividing line or are distributed evenly around a center. Simple forms of centering and symmetry can already be seen in the earliest drawings of 3- and 4-year-olds who draw two children, side-by-side, with a ball between them to indicate that they are playing. Going beyond the early simple forms of symmetry, children begin to pay attention to the size of the major figures; they create pairs of the same size or same gender and alternate such pairs within a more richly structured configuration. Symmetry in the repetition of pair formation introduces rhythm into the drawing or painting which benefits from a new attention to the equal spacing among figures and a similar distance from the edges of the page. To the extent that decorative motifs are included in the composition, repetition of the same or similar designs enriches the drawing or painting which gains in expressive power (see Figures 18a–b; see also 9c; 11b; 12a; 13a; 15c).

Figure 18 *Symmetry*
Figure 18a *Family. Boy, age 9*

Figure 18b *Orchard. Girl, age 12*

Older children tend to go beyond a very simple design that is based on a strict symmetry of the elements; they expand the scope of symmetry by introducing more complex designs that maintain spatial order and meaning with more varied items. The innovation lies in a composition of items that no longer relies on a strict one-to-one correspondence or duplication of the elements. A more dynamic form of symmetry may be achieved by, for example, drawing a large item on one side of the center line to be balanced on the other side by a group of smaller, perhaps even different items. An item placed high on the page exerts more perceived weight than one that is situated in the center or the bottom of the page, and thus differences in size and location can create a dynamic interplay between major elements. Varying the size, shape, color, and position of items in a manner that balances the individual elements enhances the meaning of the work and its aesthetic appeal. Not every youngster attains this form of complex symmetry which is mostly found among the older, highly motivated and talented children. Among the latter we also find the cartoonists who specialize in visual narratives, and tell a story in a series of frames that employ a dynamic form of symmetry (see Figures 19a–d on the following pages and Plate 2 on p.66).

Figure 19 *Dynamic Form of Symmetry*
Figure 19a *Landscape of trees and lake. Boy, age 12*

Figure 19b *Pond. Girl, age 12*

Figure 19c *Tornado. Boy, 6 years 6 months*

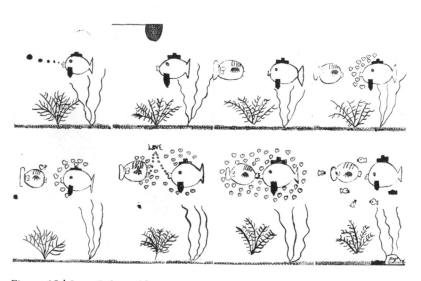

Figure 19d *Love. Girl, age 12*

Over the course of a few years, we have seen tremendous progress in the ability to depict a scene, to group items by size, shape, color, location, distance, and/or activity, important strategies for the representation of meaningful connections. These strategies impose some cohesion on a composition whose objects are drawn as independent units, each one depicted in its most characteristic format with but little attention to a central viewpoint. Gradually, however, local viewpoints make an appearance, and when a theme calls for a social interaction the protagonists tend to be drawn facing each other, indicating a partial coordination of viewpoint in one sector of the drawing.

Overall, compositional development proceeds from multiple local graphic solutions, in which each object is an independent unit, through partially coordinated mixed views, to varying degrees of interdependence, and eventually to a more unitary conception that dominates the composition. Despite the growing competence to create aesthetically pleasing and meaningful compositions, progress in the integration of all the elements of a composition is slow. A unitary conception that organizes all the elements into a coherent whole is rarely achieved during childhood and adolescence and is well beyond the horizons of child art.

Motivation, color, and the expression of feelings

In the previous sections I have emphasized the eagerness and the determination with which children develop graphic models for humans, animals, plants and, as the need arises, for such man-made objects as houses, tables, chairs, cars, swing-sets and many more. The power to create something where previously there was only a blank page, and the drive to populate the space with recognizable creatures of his or her invention testify to the intelligence that underlies artistic development from its very beginnings.

But drawings and paintings are not merely problem-solving exercises; they are expressive statements about what one knows, feels, and wants to understand. The challenges inherent in depiction and the desire to express feelings and thoughts are the master motives that inspire the many drawings and paintings produced during the childhood years. Drawing children are not only inventors of a pictorial vocabulary, they are motivated to tell a story, to give expression to their experiences, to the joys, sorrows, fears, struggles, victories and defeats of their daily lives. The childhood years are emotionally intense years where feelings of dependency and rebellion coexist, and resentment and rivalry can dominate the emotional landscape. The motivation to create on a previously blank page a pictorial world—real and imaginary—draws on deeply felt desires, fantasies, and wishes that endow the maker with a sense of power to make and to unmake, to create and to obliterate at will. For many children drawing provides an avenue for the expression of feelings in both direct and indirect ways, and some experience an urge to draw on a daily basis. The drawings depict a range of events, everyday as well as extraordinary ones that affect the child, the family, and beyond it the wider community.

In childhood, and for years to come, the family is a major source of intense feelings, of cravings for comfort and love, of generosity and empathy, but also of the painful emotions of anger, aggression, guilt, jealousy, and fear of abandonment. It is not surprising that the family is a commonly portrayed theme in drawings that are often presented as a gift for a parent or sibling accompanied by declarations of "I love you very much," "I miss you," "get better soon," "I am sorry, mom." Other drawings depict a person in bed with the caption "get better soon," two siblings holding hands with the older one declaring "don't worry, I hold your hand." The emotions that propel such a drawing are not always visible in the final product of the young whose figures are simple and not well differentiated. We can, however, learn a great deal by listening to the spontaneous comments children make when drawing; they tell us much of the thoughts and emotions that underlie their drawing, especially about such dramatic events as pregnancy, the birth of a sibling, hospitalization, divorce and its impact on the children, of the death of a pet or family member. Fears of death and attack by invaders are quite common from the age of 4 years on, but their expression is often indirect. Even less dramatic events, such as the experience of a powerful parent, can find expression as in 4-year-old Jessica's drawing of her mother and her ongoing commentary: "Mom gets mad when I am bad. We talk about being bad…I have to make big fingers, mommy uses her big hand when I am bad…" (see Figures 20a–e on pp.73–5 and Plate 3 on p.66).

Plate 1 *Child Art Blossoms: Color, Expression, and Love of Ornamentation*
Plate 1a *Twins in a bassinet. Equal size circles for head and body. Girl, age 5 years 11 months. From the collection of Malka Haas*

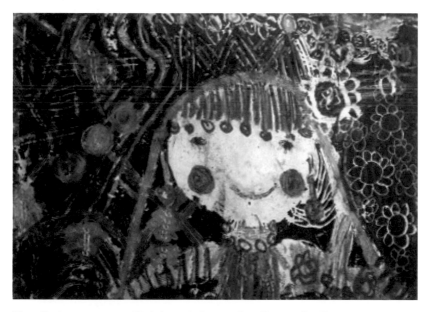

Plate 1b *An imaginary world. Girl, age 6–7. From the collection of Malka Haas*

Plate 2 *Dynamic Form of Symmetry. The scarecrow, slightly off center, is balanced by the number of brightly colored pumpkins and birds. Also, note the colorful strokes that unite foreground, middle-ground, and background in this composition. Girl, age 9*

Plate 3 *Expression of Feelings. Chickenpox. Girl, age 5*

Plate 4 *Individual Differences in Child Art Style. Expressive tendency—The warrior.*
Boy, age 6. From the collection of Malka Haas

Plate 5 *Color and Ornament in the Expressive Child Art Style*
Plate 5a *A balance between figural and ornamental tendencies. Girl, age 6.*
From the collection of Malka Haas

Plate 5b *Ornamental qualities dominate this imaginative and colorful portrait. Girl, age 7. From the collection of Malka Haas*

Plate 5c *From the land of the fairytale:"I am flying, I love it." Girl, age 7*

Plate 5d *Animals on land and sea. Girl, age 7*

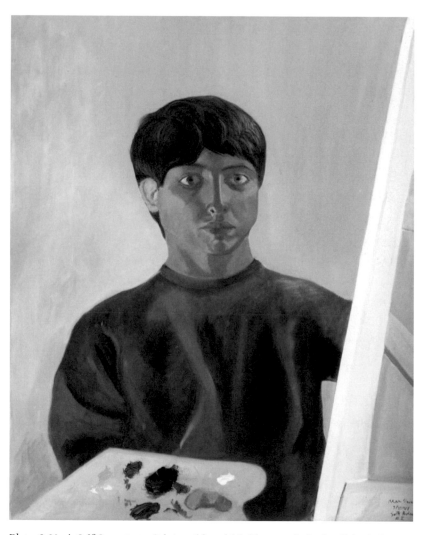

Plate 6 *Max's Self-Portraits in Oil. Ages 10 and 12. Photography by Eve Golomb-Leavitt*
Plate 6a

Plate 6b

Plate 7 *Antonia's Self-Portrait in Oil. Color plays a central role in this portrait. Age 16.*

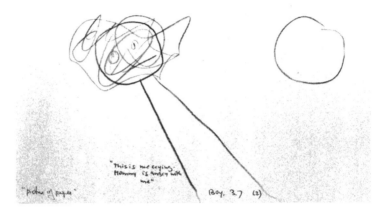

Figure 20 *Expression of Feelings*
Figure 20a *"This is me crying." Boy, 3 years 7 months*

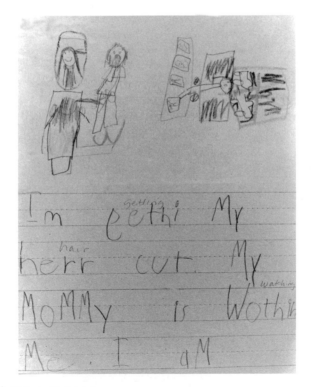

Figure 20b *Haircut. Girl, age 6*

Figure 20c *Nightmare. Girl, 7 years 10 months*

Figure 20d *Family Breakup. Girl, age 12*

Figure 20e *Mother. "Mom gets mad when I am bad." Note the exaggerated size of the right arm and the two feet. Girl, age 4*

The family continues to play a significant role as the child's environment extends beyond the early caretakers, which frequently occurs with attendance at a daycare center; somewhat later the school gains in importance, with teachers, friends and bullies, themes of beauty contests, sports competition, and trophies moving center place. Friendship and social exclusion, popularity and stardom are highly emotional themes that find expression, either directly or more indirectly, in the drawings of the middle childhood years. Fear and aggression embodied in the drawings of monsters and witches by the younger children make way for robbers, gangsters, imprisonment, star wars, accidents, and topics derived from the comics and TV. We note significant gender differences in the selection of a theme with boys fascinated by more aggressive topics including such jokes as "hanging the teachers," or "exploding the school," and girls often focused on more social and tranquil settings, and hints of romance.

What are the pictorial means children employ to express their emotions and what changes can we observe with age and experience? Let us consider, in turn, the role of the theme, the selection of expressive characteristics, the use of color, and the style of representation.

Theme

To begin with, it is the theme which the child chooses that is the main carrier of the dominant emotion. In many cases, the subject matter of a drawing and its simple composition convey the intended meaning quite well as seen in a birthday party that features balloons, a cake, and presents (see Figure 10b); in a joke about juggling apples; in a drawing of a sad child with tears running down its cheeks and a broken toy on the floor; in a drawing of a sick child lying in bed; in a drawing of a group of children playing together and one child at a distance suggesting exclusion (see Figures 21a–b).

Figure 21 *Theme as Carrier of Meaning*
Figure 21a *Joke: juggling apples. Boy, 5 years 9 months*

Figure 21b *Sick in the hospital. Boy, age 9*

In cases that involve complex emotions, the child may not fully understand the range of feelings embedded in the scene just created that includes items he cannot quite understand how they got into the picture. The painting may capture the general mood of the scene, although the content is only vaguely understood and poorly verbalized by the drawer, perhaps an adaptive response to a painful situation. An example can be found in Varda's drawing of a black woman and her commentary on it as a young adult:

> I see myself standing in front of a big white sheet of paper...and I begin to work. I take a wide brush, dip it into paint, and on the white paper arises the large figure of a black woman. The black woman grows, surrounded by decorative ornaments and symbols of great beauty. Below her feet, at the bottom of the page, I add a little grave of the child who died, over which the black woman weeps. How did she get onto my paper? Over whom did I grieve when I was 10 years old? What feelings were stirred up in me that here appear in my painting?[2]

This anecdotal account gives us a glimpse of the all-involving act of artistic creation, the total bodily, visual, and mental engagement.

Depiction of mood

While the theme and its composition are intimately linked and able to convey meaning in a general way, the ability to graphically depict the mood of the protagonists evolves only gradually, with the head or the face singled out as the carrier of the experienced emotion. Thus, happiness, sadness, and anger are portrayed by changes in the drawing of the mouth with an upward curving line depicting a smiling face, a downward curve sadness, while anger may be shown in a set of prominently displayed teeth, a straight or zigzag line for the mouth, and somewhat later also in the diagonal slashes of the eyebrows (see Figures 22a–b).

Figure 22 *Depiction of Happiness, Sadness, and Anger*
Figure 22a *Girl, 7 years 11 months*

Figure 22b *Girl, 11 years 9 months*

Changes in posture that are typical of the experienced emotion, for example, of happiness, sadness, or anger, occur infrequently in the younger children whose figures are mostly presented in the preferred frontal view, upright standing and motionless. Even the older children are conservative in terms of the body's posture and tend to use verbal commentary to augment the message. With few exceptions, notably the direction of the arms, the body's posture remains rather static. An effective way to convey emotion is often attained by exaggerating the form and size of various body parts, especially the head which can yield striking compositions. The use of energetic brush strokes, choice of primary colors, and an emphasis on symmetry all tend to heighten the expressive power of a drawing or painting (see Plate 4, p.67).

The role of color

Since from an early age children have color preferences, what is the role of color in their drawings, especially in expressing emotion? As we have previously seen, the preschoolers' first drawing efforts are focused on the creation of recognizable forms, but once they attain a degree of mastery over the basic shapes, 4- and 5-year-olds begin to color in the outlined forms, and color becomes increasingly important in their enjoyment of art making. One can see a progression from using colors somewhat idiosyncratically, from the sheer pleasure in primary and contrasting hues, to outlining humans and animals with a single color and, eventually, a realistic adherence to colors that define well-known items, for example, the sun and moon in yellow, the ocean or lake in blue, tree trunks in brown, and the grass green. From, approximately, the age of 6 years the tendency is to use local true color: red lips, blue or brown eyes, blond or dark hair, body contour in either black or orange to simulate skin color. In the middle childhood years "realistic colors" become the rule for most of the drawings and paintings, and brilliant colors begin to dominate the composition and are intimately linked to the aesthetic experience of the artist.

Are colors indicative of the mood of the child artist? It has often been assumed that there is a natural connection between colors and specific emotions in child art, and that the selection of colors might offer a window into the child's mood and feelings. Colors play such an important role in our experience of the world and verbal language suggests many linkages between color and emotion as in the expression of "feeling blue" to indicate sadness or depression and "seeing red" to state anger. Given cultural differences in the connection between colors and emotions, for example, the color white stands for purity in some societies and for mourning in others, it is perhaps not surprising that in my studies of children's drawings I did not find any indication of color coding for the expression of the major emotions.[3] However, darker colors tend to characterize themes that portray a negative mood, while bright colors occur more frequently in happy compositions.

Individual differences

Finally I want to address individual differences in the preferred style of child artists who convey their feelings in contrasting ways. To use a broad generalization, we can observe two different trends in children's motivation for art making: a narrative tendency and an expressive tendency, both of which are influenced by the cultural context in which the art is produced. The narrative tendency is motivated by the desire to tell a story, to convey information about the nature and function of objects and the actions and intentions of the protagonists. This motivation drives the desire for narrative competence; it calls for differentiating and coordinating the diverse elements of the composition and it aims for naturalism in art (see Figure 23).

The expressive tendency tends to violate naturalism in the selection of forms and colors that convey the dominant emotion, often by exaggerating the size and colors of body parts and assigning a greater role to decorative elements in a composition. Color and ornamentation hold a special attraction for these child artists (see Plate 4 on p.67 and Plates 1a and b on p.63). Here I also want to mention visual narratives, depicting a theme over several frames that move the protagonists across time and space in the tradition of cartoons, a style that can effectively convey the theme and its emotional significance (see Figure 19d). In the case of girls, such themes may take on the character of a fairytale while boys' fantasy narratives often center on warfare and, frequently, are presented in an extensive series of drawings. Such artists tend to create an imaginary world, a paracosmos where good and evil are starkly represented, where evil powers always challenge the good ones and need to be vanquished time and again.

Figure 23 *Individual Differences in Child Art Style. Narrative Tendency and Naturalism. The hunter. Boy, age 6*

I have stressed that drawings are meaningful actions that play an important role in the child's creation of real and imaginary worlds. They are playful actions that at times employ deliberate distortions, jokes, and elements of fantasy, but they are also expressions of a growing sense of self. Recognizing the multiple faces of child art, we need a word of caution. It is not always easy to distinguish between the drawing of a sad child and a child who is feeling sad, and the depiction of feelings does not tell us who the referent is. One ought to be careful when interpreting a drawing since a drawing is not a simple print-out of the child's heart and mind. Listening to the child's own thoughts about his or her work is of course helpful, and when given in the presence of an empathic participant observer the highly personal meaning of a drawing might be understood, which is often the case in a psychotherapeutic context. In general, one should be aware that drawings do not lend themselves to a simple reading that has diagnostic validity.

Drawings of mentally handicapped children

What do we know about the drawings of mentally handicapped children and how do they compare with the drawings of normally developing youngsters? In studies of children whose intellectual development is delayed we find that their drawings resemble those of younger ones and thus do not deviate from the normal course I have sketched so far. However, since they are older than the normally developing children of comparable mental level, they may have had more experience in drawing and tend to include more detail in their work. As they get older, some mentally handicapped individuals develop their artistic sensibility in the framework of a supportive environment and create beautiful paintings and tapestry reminiscent of child and folk art. This work has often been termed "outsider art" and found an appreciative audience.

An exception to the above-mentioned mentally handicapped children are some autistic youngsters who have shown an extraordinary skill and artistic talent in their drawings. Although mentally retarded and language delayed, these children display great artistry in their work; the most well-known among them is Nadia, who between the ages of 4 and 7 years drew remarkable pictures of animals and some humans, drawings reminiscent of some adult graphic artists.[4] Other equally accomplished mentally handicapped as well as autistic artists are Steven Wiltshire and Richard Wawro whose work has been exhibited to much acclaim. I would like to point out that these are exceptional cases and that the majority of autistic children and adults draw at a level that reflects their mental development.[5]

Artistically gifted children

In the preceding sections I have highlighted the creativity of young children who invent spontaneously and without any training a pictorial language that is unique, personally meaningful, and yet recognizable across different times and places. Unlike the spoken language for which the human environment provides ready-made models, young children invent a graphic symbol system for which their culture does not provide a sample that can be imitated, and in that sense each child is an original artist. For most children, the effort to develop this pictorial language is intrinsically satisfying and, where the conditions are favorable, art making is pursued throughout the childhood years.

In outlining change and progress in the development of child art I have focused on general patterns that are typical for ordinary, normally developing children. But what is the role of talent, and can we identify those youngsters who show a special gift for drawing or painting? What are some of the similarities and differences that characterize the talented and set them apart from ordinary children who love art making?

In order to identify children who are gifted in an artistic or intellectual domain, it is generally useful to consider their achievements in relation to their peers.[6,7] In child art, children are labeled "gifted" or "talented" when their drawings are considerably more advanced than that of their age mates. This can take a number of different forms: it includes drawings that at an early age employ advanced naturalistic techniques, as well as drawings that adhere to the flat child art style but display originality, inventiveness, expressive power, vibrant colors, and ornamental qualities reminiscent of folk art.

In the first case are the "realists," children who show an early technical mastery in the use of line, rotation of figures, and three-quarter views. These youngsters capture the contours of humans and animals in a naturalistic style, employ partial overlap of forms, oblique lines, cross-hatching, and foreshortening, all of which suggest the solidity of an object extended in space. These young realists are motivated to capture the appearance of objects and scenes with fidelity and singularity of purpose. Their precocity is quite striking and they tend to be seen as child prodigies (see Figures 24a–f).

Figure 24 *Eitan: A Precociously Gifted Realist*
Figure 24a *Cement truck, 2 years 7 months*

Figure 24b *Car, 3 years 9 months*

Figure 24c *View of Jerusalem, 4 years 2 months*

Figure 24d *Cement truck, 4 years 4 months*

Figure 24e *Construction scene, 5 years 2 months*

Figure 24f *Near-accident, 6 years 6 months*

Unlike the realists, the colorists develop their work within the two-dimensional child art style and, unconcerned with anatomical fidelity, use dramatic rather than naturalistic forms. They adopt a more painterly style and relish the expressive and decorative attributes of color, texture, and design; their richly ornamental works are strikingly appealing and reminiscent of folk art (see Plates 5a–d on pp.67–9). Other artistically talented youngsters favor visual narratives that cast their characters in a series of time frames based on the cartoon format. These talented children can be quite passionate about the heroes and villains they have created, their triumph and tribulation; at times their visual narratives can extend over several years. Such intense involvement over months and years is not limited to visual narratives in drawing, and a similar commitment can be found in modeling a series of well-identified figures in clay or pipe cleaners (see Figure 25). The expert modelers can create multiple families, clans, or tribes of imaginary creatures, animal, humanoid or robotic, and keep track of their genealogy and kinship over several generations. In these cases the relationship of the artist to his or her creation is akin to imaginative make-believe play (see a description of Brittney's paracosmos in Chapter 2).

Figure 25a–f *Brittney's Imaginary World. Age 14–15*
Figure 25a

Figure 25b

Figure 25c

Figure 25d

Figure 25e

Figure 25f

Across their different pursuits, the talented are singled out for their precocity in the acquisition of technical drawing skills and/or their early awareness of artistic form and quality. They do not skip the typical stages in drawing development but develop their skills more rapidly and more fully which makes their work artistically distinct. As we have seen, there are marked individual differences in the stylistic preferences of talented children, their chosen topics, preferred medium, and their intense motivation to draw and paint. But there are also commonalities in their urge to draw and paint, to create their stories, to master the depiction of the objects and protagonists they feel so strongly about, to teach themselves what they need to know and what they wish to express. These are the children who draw on a daily basis and spend hours focused on their project. What they have in common is a heightened awareness of the visual world, superior visual memory, visual-spatial motor precocity, sensitivity to line and composition, color and ornament. At a relatively early age they may show a special sensitivity to the changing appearance of a scene during different times of the day, delight in the beauty of a sunset, and try to capture the image for its texture and specialness. They are likely to use visual metaphors more effectively than their less talented age mates.

To provide a more concrete picture of the role drawing or painting can play in the life of a talented child, I present two sketches of children who have drawn extensively since their earliest years, and whose works fit the description of talent previously discussed.

Portrait of Max, a young artist

Max S. is a 14-year-old boy who has drawn throughout his childhood although he mostly remembers his work from the fourth grade on. His family is artistically talented, his father graduated from art school, and Max is the youngest of three graphically talented children.

The earliest drawings that he seems to remember are drawings of cats and a drawing about a boat and a fisherman, with the landscape sketched in. They are attractive drawings and probably date from the age of 6–7; in style and composition they are quite typical of this age group. Max reports that his father has been his earliest teacher who taught him drawing and painting and continues to do so. From age 9 years he has also received lessons at the museum school and this continues till today. When Max was 10 years old, his father registered both of them at a studio with nude models where Max was the only child among the attending adults. Indeed, his sketchbooks are filled with competent drawings of the human figure, mostly nudes, interspersed with portraits of his father and they attest to the value the father places on mastering figure drawings. Indeed, his drawings show that he has mastered three-dimensional techniques far in advance of his age mates, and his figures are lively and animated (see Figure 26). In addition to drawing, Max also paints with oils and the striking self-portraits from the age of 10 and 12 show how much he has gained in representational skills and the application of color (see Plates 6a and 6b on pp.70–1). In recent times, with the encouragement of his father, he is branching out and has painted more abstract geometric compositions. Max is also interested in three-dimensional work, and with the help from a sculptor-welder he has learned to work with scrap metal and constructed attractive abstract sculptures that adorn the front of the house.

Figure 26 *Max's Figure Drawing. Age 10–11*

Max's identity is wrapped up with being an artist, and this has been the case since fourth or fifth grade. He always has a small notebook at hand and draws almost continuously. During class time he is compulsive about drawing in the margins; he has to move his fingers and teachers have come to accept this behavior. He is a good student— when he cares—when he can translate a task, an assignment, into something visual. In some parts of math where visualization is not relevant he has more trouble.

From the age of 9 years Max has copied models of artists he likes and admires and currently he is very much influenced by Matisse. In all his artistic endeavors he is fully supported by his parents who provide him with professional instruction during the school year, art camp in the summer, visits to museums in Boston and New York, and display his artwork throughout the house. Altogether, he has received intense training and lessons from his father who acts as teacher and critic, providing guidance as well as professional training at the museum school. His relationship with his father is very close and he is grateful for his help.

Max thinks of himself as "weird." He elaborates that he does not like sports and is not good at it; he is unconventional and can do outlandish things with his friends. He seems self-assured, is verbally very articulate and reflective of his work and the progress he has made, and notes that meditation, which he has taken up jointly with his father, has a beneficial effect on him and his artwork. He plans to attend Cooper Union in New York; perhaps he will become a designer of toys, an idea he finds attractive.

Antonia D., portrait of a young artist

Antonia is a 16-year-old high-school student whose major is studio art. As far as she can remember she has always liked to draw and paint, and create sculptures from all kinds of found objects. A drawing from the age of 5 years depicts the large, colorful and expressive figure of a dragon flying over a village situated at the sea. It is an exuberant example of child art of an imaginative child who made up stories and created diverse make-believe identities for herself as a dog, pirate, princess, or Aladdin. She loved to collect abandoned objects, search for "trash" and then build a fort in her backyard.

Until Antonia reached high school she was essentially self-taught since private lessons were beyond her reach. There seems to be interest in and talent for the arts in her family; her mother likes to paint with watercolors and would love to take art courses, and Antonia's older sister also has a talent for drawing. Due to economic concerns, there is not much support in the family for a career in the arts. Antonia too has some hesitation about a profession that may not guarantee her a good standard of living. However, art making has always provided her with deep satisfaction; she has always preferred art making over other activities, and it continues to be her favorite pastime. When she works on an art project she can concentrate on it for long periods of time quite unlike her approach to other tasks, such as homework, where her work is intermittent. She describes herself as having an overactive mind that "goes a mile a minute" and art making relaxes her, it has a calming effect. When she is involved in a drawing or painting she can focus totally; for a prolonged period of time she does not think of anything besides the different phases of her project and enjoys planning all the detailed steps that bring it to completion. This may take a week or two and, of course, at the end of it there is a product which is also very rewarding.

Figure 27 *Antonia's Portrait at 16. In her pencil drawings she emphasizes detail and focuses on the facial features*

Over the last few years Antonia has become a fine portraitist, working with pencils and pen that allow for the precision she aims for (see Figure 27). When done in black and white the emphasis is on getting the features right, to capture the uniqueness of the face, its subtle aspects. But color is also important, at times even a dominant factor for the expression of feelings that go into a painting. About her self-portrait, Antonia notes: "the personality is me and the contrasting colors, for example of blue and yellow-orange represent the different sides of the person, both are me." The use of color strengthens the portrait by giving it greater depth and complexity beyond the expression of the facial features (see Plate 7 on p.72). But color is also important in landscapes, and the use of colors that go beyond the natural scene can convey a special mood or feeling for the place. For example, the blues and black in an urban scene can convey a mood even if people are absent. For painting Antonia prefers oil and multiple layers of strong colors. She does not name her paintings or sculpture since it would not capture all that goes into an artwork. She feels no need to analyze her feelings, the importance for her lies in the expression she creates. She is passionate about her work and has a special affinity for working with clay and found objects.

Although she loves drawing and painting, her greatest attraction is to sculpture. If time permits, she prefers sculpture over all else, especially working with found objects, but the construction of a sculpture is very demanding and more time consuming. She hopes in the future to devote the time that sculpture requires and to acquire the skills that will enable her to work in this medium.

Her work in different media speaks of an openness and originality, an ability to commit to demanding projects that are the mark of a young artist. There is much room for growth as an artist and for finding a niche that might be able to sustain her over time. At this point she plans to pursue a liberal arts degree with a strong emphasis on the visual arts.[8]

The two young artists whose profile I have presented seem determined to pursue art as a lifelong endeavor. To what extent does childhood giftedness predict future artistic development and the choice of one's career? We know from the life histories of well-known artists that they were ardent drawers and painters as children, but the reverse is not the case and not many gifted child artists pursue a career in the arts, and an even smaller number can claim success, financial or otherwise, as a practicing artist. As usual, there are many reasons for this state of affairs. With adolescence and the broadening of social and cultural outlets, new opportunities arise that invite the youngsters to test their skills and interests and consider alternatives. Parents and other significant people in the adolescent's life may also urge him or her to consider the financial prospects in the life of an artist and the uncertainties of such a profession. Furthermore, the intense emotions that have been a driving factor in the earlier years may have diminished or found another outlet. Regardless of the choice of a career, the talented children gain immensely from their intense dedication to their chosen art form which leads to an enhanced sense of self, pride in their accomplishments, and the social benefits that come with the high regard of others.

The socio-cultural milieu

What is the role of culture in the identification and nurturing of talent in the visual arts and, more broadly speaking, for artistic development in general? To begin with the primary conditions for art making, children need materials, an assortment of paper, clay, pencils, charcoal, magic markers, crayons, paint, brushes, and other items that are the basic tools which the culture, in the role of parent or teacher, provides. Although the urge to create forms is a universal one, and the beginnings of artistic development are similar across different communities, as children become familiar with the medium and what they can produce, they are also influenced by the cultural models, the drawings in their picture books, illustrations in newspapers, etc. Thus, the drawings of young Japanese children have all the earmarks of the work of their young counterparts in Western societies. We find the typical tadpole figures and their descendents, but we also note some of the characteristic features that derive from their popular cartoon characters, such as large eyes, tiny noses, and broad somewhat flattened heads (see Figures 28a–b).

Figure 28a–b *Drawings of Japanese Children. Girls, ages 4 and 5*
Figure 28a

Figure 28b

During the middle childhood years, their familiarity with and love of well-known cartoon characters (manga) and their reproduction finds expression in very skillful drawings of actors drawn in diverse poses, viewed from a variety of perspectives, a technical competence far in advance of the art of the average Western child. Likewise, Chinese children, from the early school years on, are exposed to explicit teachings of the basic shapes of an assortment of flowers, birds, shrimps, and other items and their general drawing ability is in advance of that of their age mates in the West. Clearly, the socio-cultural environment and its values have a significant effect on the manner in which child art finds its expression.

This brings me to the topic of "copying." In general, children are only able to copy what they understand and complex drawings, especially those in perspective, are beyond the ability of most children and of many adults as well. However, the kind of drawings that are only one or two steps above the level of the child's own drawings and understanding may well serve as a model to be aspired to. Some children, especially the ones who love the comics and try their hands at visual narratives, benefit from extensive practice and visual feedback, copying from a model until they have gained sufficient competence. If a child wants to copy from a model, there is no harm in such an action, provided it is his or her desire and helps master some new and desirable techniques. Does copying arrest the child's initiative and creativity as some have argued? If it is an aid to the child's *own* endeavors there is no good reason to discourage such an activity, especially since children will always be affected by the art they see their siblings and peers produce, and the style valued by their teachers. Artists have always learned from so-called copying, and the main reason educators have warned against it is from fear that it will distort the child's own search for—and discovery of—solutions that can lead to true understanding and a sense of accomplishment. For adolescents who are gifted drawers, extensive copying of models leads to highly skilled performance, and is congruent with their ambition is to master this medium.

As children reach the end of their childhood years, the cultural models become more dominant and tend to define the goals toward which the artist is aspiring. In Western cultures, the emphasis has been on mastering realism in art which requires extensive training for all but the most talented children who may well be able, on their own, to analyze the models and to infer the principles that underlie their construction. For most children, the difficulty in reaching an acceptable level of realism in their drawings diminishes their enthusiasm for art making and foretells the end of a highly productive and creative period in their childhood. The attraction of computer games, of photography, and the impact of cultural values may also play a role in the diminished attention to art instruction which, unlike music, is infrequently pursued outside the school system.

The end of child art

I have described artistic development as a problem-solving and emotionally satisfying activity that puts the child in charge of a universe of his own creation and leaves a tangible, visible record of his thoughts and feeling. I have highlighted the universal nature of the milestones of child art expressed in the drawings of ordinary, talented, and mentally handicapped children, and across widely diverse cultures. With age and practice those children who love to draw and paint and who continue to devote much time and effort to their work will have gained the ability to attend to multiple tasks, that is, to plan, monitor, critically review, and revise the emerging representation.

Artistic development, in the absence of training, is a spontaneous process that flourishes during the childhood years and attains its aesthetic highpoint around the ages of 8 or 9 years, after which it tends to reach a plateau. It is during the elementary school years that we note a gradual decline in the rate of spontaneous art productions, and for many children it signals the end of a very creative and productive period in child art. There are likely to be diverse reasons and competing interests that underlie the decline of artistic activity, and with the widening horizons of middle childhood new outlets for self-expression can be found in sports, dance, music, chess, computer games, and the opportunities for social activities. For some children, the technical problems associated with more advanced pictorial strategies spell the end of their artistic explorations. Others continue their involvement and strive to transform the flat child art style in their desire for greater naturalism. For many children their early experience with art making has laid the foundation for an enduring appreciation of the arts and some will take it up again in adulthood, as a hobby or even a serious endeavor.

The art of child art

Earlier I raised the question whether child art ought to be considered "art" and when we consult with educators, artists, and art historians we find wide divergences of opinion. Some have stressed commonalities between child and adult art and point to the significance art making holds for both, the extended time commitment devoted to their work, the intensity and sincerity of the emotion that is reminiscent of the adult artist, and in many cases continuity in an adult artist's theme, style, and elaboration that date from the childhood years. Among the most ardent admirers of child art were some of the prominent modern artists of the early 20th century who were deeply influenced by children's artwork on which they modeled many of their paintings and drawings. These artists, inspired by what they conceived to be the truthfulness and spontaneity of children's work and vision, its freedom from conventions, its sincerity and directness, favored the flatness of pictorial space, simplification of form and their distortion, and the use of primary contrasting colors.[9]

If the curiosity, inventiveness, and emotional intensity of children who devote much time and effort to their art is reminiscent of the adult artist, there are of course also fundamental differences between them. The simplicity of child art reflects the naivety of beginners, the child's limited understanding of pictorial possibilities and alternative forms of representation. Unlike the child, adults have access to a large repertoire of representational styles, and their choice of using some forms that resemble child art is a deliberate act of rejecting artistic conventions, and a search for new modes of expression. Above all, child art is a-historical, it is unconcerned with artistic traditions or conventions, it does not break with custom, it is self-contained and self-limiting and reaches its natural endpoint at the end of the childhood years.

Despite significant changes in the styles of 20th-century art, child art has continued to inspire artists who have been enamored of different phases of children's work: the abstract expressionists of the post-World War II period lauded the spontaneity and beauty of the easel painting of 4- and 5-year-olds, while a later generation found inspiration in the cartoons of older children, a clear illustration that art and art appreciation are grounded in a socio-cultural context. What in previous periods was viewed as "primitive" and intellectually immature or even defective appears to the contemporary observer a sign of creativity, inventiveness, and playfulness. From this perspective, the beauty of child art lies in its simplicity and directness, its ability to engage the viewer with its simple lines and irregular contours, its disproportionate figures and bright unmixed colors that evoke an unmediated emotional response.

Child art has flourished where tools are made available and where this activity is valued. In this art form the child can be seen as the creator of a first and basic pictorial vocabulary but also as a participant in a peer culture, and a member of a wider community that promulgates certain views of art. Art making occurs in a cultural context, it is always the product of effort and training, and those youngsters who aspire to become artists will increasingly gear their training toward the mastery of skills valued in their chosen field.

2

Play: A Wellspring of the Imagination

When we think about play many different activities come to mind and the word calls forth images of playing a musical instrument, a game of chess, poker, bridge, or other card games, team sports, enacting or narrating a play, musical, or pageant. All of these diverse activities are forms of entertainment that fulfill a significant role in the social life of a community. Some historians have identified play and its rituals as crucial elements of human civilization, its creative source from which poetry, music, drama, dance, and religion derive. While the word "play" applies broadly across diverse domains, it also brings to mind puppies and kittens chasing a ball and, most vividly, images of children at play with their toys, creating and recreating scenes from their daily life or their imagination.

It is not easy to define the concept of play since the term applies to such diverse activities. If one juxtaposes play with the concept of work-as-a-serious-endeavor, play appears as a voluntary-spontaneous activity that is self-initiated and enjoyable, with rules that are flexible and somewhat relaxed, an activity that is an end in itself, and not means-end oriented toward the creation of a useful product. Such a distinction between play and work does not hold under all conditions; witness sports games that are highly professional, rule governed, demanding, and potentially lucrative; likewise, practicing a musical instrument is a time-consuming activity that requires following an explicit set of rules. However, when we focus on child play, the distinction between tasks imposed by an adult and activities freely and spontaneously chosen by the child who decides what to play, when, and for how long is helpful. Among the many activities that fall under the heading of "play" such as building with blocks or legos, constructing puzzles, assembling toys, hide and seek, and many others, I am going to focus on imaginative or pretend play, the youngster's invention of a make-believe world where the actors and their props undergo a magical transformation. In make-believe play the child adopts a new identity, a role borrowed from real-life models or invented ones, assigns roles to his or her partners, and as the need arises transforms objects to serve the pretense theme. This is a highly complex mental activity where the playing child maintains a dual orientation toward the pretense theme and the real situation, for example, pretending that a piece of clay is a birthday cake with candles, offering everyone a piece of the cake, going through the motion of pretend tasting, nibbling, and lauding the cake without confusing the pretend and real identity of the clay blob which would mean taking a real bite out of the "cake."

The origin of this ability to momentarily transform the real world, the self and its relationship with significant others emerges surprisingly early, during the second year of life, a period during which the child seems wholly focused on the physical world, propelled to master walking, climbing, opening and closing doors and drawers, eager to manipulate objects and discover what can be done with them. It is during this period that we also see the beginnings of pretense play as a mental, somewhat subversive activity that will have implications for the child's emotional, cognitive, and social development. Of course, imaginary scenarios play a role throughout the lifecycle, and in the case of individuals talented in this domain, they may become writers, actors and/or film directors.

Given its early and universal appearance in children's development the question arises as to its function and the underlying motivations that drive pretense play activities for years to come. Many authors point to the dependency of the child, its powerlessness vis-à-vis the adults who control his or her world, the desire to change unwelcome outcomes, to exact revenge on competitors, to punish the perpetrators of evil deeds, to exercise power and create a more accommodating world. In pretense, many negative emotions can be expressed without running the risk of retaliation for aggression or being shamed for regressive fantasies, and in this sense it is a protected and safe domain perhaps beneficial for learning how to modulate emotions. Beyond this list that emphasizes the many negative experiences of the child, there is also a desire to restore balance and assure forgiveness and, equally important, to understand the adult world by enacting the role of parent, teacher or other significant figures, a rehearsal for future roles. There is pleasure in the enactment of known scenarios, in remaking the world to one's liking and, eventually, in the invention of worlds as yet untried, of sheer whimsy and imagination. At the heart of pretense or make-believe play and its diverse scenarios is the adoption of a role that is *enacted* and this distinguishes it from pure fantasy where an altered identity may be imagined and indulged in without an overt action.

I now turn to an account of the antecedents of pretense play, its evolution during the childhood years, and the role it can play in the child's social, cognitive, and emotional development.

Antecedents and the emergence of pretense behavior

The world of make-believe, of pretending to be someone other than your real self, does not appear full blown but has antecedents we can trace. It is toward the end of his first year of life that an infant engages in many acts that can be classified as "playful," playing games of peek-a-boo with a caring adult, pat-a-cake, clapping his hands in response to a partner's action, waving bye-bye, dropping or throwing objects from a crib or playpen and expecting an adult to oblige and return the toy, to be dropped once again. These simple games are acts of mutual imitation, a coordination of sight, sound, and motor action, accompanied by smiles and laughter that signal the delight of the participants.

The infant also develops what can best be called "rituals," a sequence of actions that is routinely adhered to in familiar situations. For example, during bath time a toddler may insist on the selection of toys he or she takes with him, the order in which they create a big splash before they are dispatched outside the tub. Many children develop a ceremonial set of actions that are followed at bedtime. Jean Piaget,[10] who was a great observer of his own children's early years, reported on a play ritual that bordered on make-believe. Upon going to sleep, Jacqueline had developed a ritual which she observed nightly: first she lay down on her side, next came sucking her thumb, which was followed by getting hold of the fringe of her pillow, an ordered series of actions that preceded falling asleep. At age 9 months, Jacqueline was sitting in her cot playing with her toys when one of her actions reminded her of what she usually did before going to sleep. This initiated a repetition of the usual actions: lying down on her side, holding on to a corner of the fringe of the pillow, and sucking her thumb. It was a short-lived imitative-play episode and she quickly resumed her previous activities. It is a nice example of a transitional phase, between mere imitation and pretense. Jacqueline clearly had no intention of going to sleep, she enacted a series of going-to-sleep behaviors taken out of their context, but since she followed the usual script, it seems to fall short of a true act of pretense which calls for some transformation of the scene. Her playful action was a precise repetition, an imitation of her routine of going to sleep, and not yet a symbolic act of pretend behavior that would indicate to herself or a playmate that the going-to-sleep action was merely make-believe. At 15 months, Jacqueline seemed to perfect her game of going-to-sleep and her behavior suggests that she was aware of the make-believe character of her actions. While exploring her toys, she noticed a cloth whose fringed edges reminded her of her pillow. This observation set the game going, namely, taking hold of the fringe, sucking her thumb while lying down on her side, rapidly blinking her eyes as if she were sleeping, all the while laughing and exclaiming: no, no!

Other forms of solitary early pretense play behavior can be seen in 18-month-old Raphi, who, seated in his highchair, moved an empty can of tuna back and forth on the table and made a loud motor noise, brm-brm, as if driving a car. Next he placed the empty can triumphantly on his head and declared that it was a "hat." These are examples of spontaneously enacted pretense behaviors in which the object's real meaning has been suppressed, momentarily, and is then transformed to serve the play theme. At first the tendency is to enact everyday familiar scenes on the self, pretend washing of hands, pretend combing of hair, pretend eating, writing, reading a newspaper, sewing. Somewhat later, often in association with an adult caretaker, such actions may be applied to a doll or a toy animal, feeding and rocking the doll as if it were a baby, brushing its hair, putting teddy to bed, talking on a pretend phone, moving a toy car along the floor and making motor noises, all examples taken from the child's everyday life experiences and often enacted jointly with an adult partner. These games as well as early solitary pretense play episodes are relatively brief and as yet do not entail role taking, for example, acting as "mommy" and interacting with a make-believe "daddy" in a jointly constructed game of pretense. While toddlers like the company of other children, they tend to play alongside each other, a parallel form of playing that does not call for much coordination of their activities. A favorite game of 2-year-olds that continues to be favored by older ones is the creation of a "house" or "tent" off limits to adults, in which a blanket is stretched over a number of chairs, or the players are hiding under a sofa and lots of pillows. It is interesting that older siblings can have a significant impact on the pretense play of their 2-year-old little brother or sister by engaging them in their make-believe play. Under these conditions even 2-year-olds can develop an unexpected competence acting the assigned role.

Beyond the pleasure of imitating diverse actions taken out of their usual context, pretense play can also serve to gain mastery over distressing events and thus to reassure the toddler, which can be glimpsed in the case of an 18-month-old little boy who happened to be Freud's grandson. For some time, he had been playing a solitary game of disappearance and retrieval, throwing a spool attached to a string into his crib followed by retrieving it, and repeating this cycle many times over. Upon retrieval, he used to exclaim "da," meaning, here you are. Freud discovered the meaning of this pretense game on a day the child's mother had left her house for a few hours. In her absence the toddler placed himself in front of a large mirror, ducked down so that his mirror image vanished and then reappeared when he stood up, which he greeted happily with a cry of "here you are." It was a game about absence and restoration, and it also shed light on the meaning of the game with the spool: his mother's absence had caused him distress, the feeling of having lost her, and by playing games of disappearance and reappearance he mastered his anxiety and reassured himself that his mother would also return.

These early pretense episodes are relatively simple and short-lived. The next few months see an increase in the number of elements the toddler introduces into a game of pretense which enlivens the play theme as the doll or the teddy bear becomes an active play and conversational partner. Between 2½ and 3 years a genuine form of symbolic play emerges.

Symbolic play

Unlike the brief, imitative form of pretense that is typical of the transitional phase, symbolic play is characterized by the transformation of the player, his or her partner, and the objects, real or imagined, that play a central role in the evolution of a theme and serve as food, medicines, dishes, blanket, vehicle, utensils, and other items as needed. Transformations of this kind rest on the capacity to evoke in thought objects that are out of sight and serve as symbols for the missing items. Symbolic thought is a mental activity that transcends the concrete perception-bound reality of the actor and the objects he or she can conjure up for the development of the play theme. Unlike the earlier sensory-motor play of the toddler or the constructive block play of the preschooler who builds elaborate structures, pretense play involves a mental action that expands the horizon of the playing child who is aware "that she is thinking it up," even though she may not be able to fully articulate it in words. For the duration of the game, the child, the partner, and the relevant objects are transformed while also maintaining their original identity. When adopting a role (mom, dad, baby, pet, policeman, robber, astronaut, pirate, king, princess, teacher, nurse, doctor, witch) and acting on it, even the preschooler does not forget his or her real identity. If need be she can momentarily step out of her role, for example, to explain the plot to her play partner or to answer her mother's call, and then return effortlessly to the pretense realm.

The same rule of dual identity of the real and the pretend self underlies also object substitution, which is an integral part of the developing plot. The child who treats a blob of play dough as if it were food carefully refrains from biting into it. In one of our studies this rule was deliberately violated when the adult play partner bit into the play dough cookie. The child was horrified and promptly declared: "you are going to die."

Substitutions are an integral part of make-believe play, and objects are usually selected because they tend to fit the subject matter. Rarely are substitutions arbitrary or incongruous, for example, pretending that a toy rabbit is a cake or a sausage, or that a postcard is a toothbrush. Pretense transformations are best performed on objects that are suitable in terms of their form and function, but neutral objects can serve as well; for example, a yellow block can represent food, perhaps cheese, while a blob of clay can stand for cake. If the substitution is unusual and violates implied norms of pretense, it may become the source of jokes, laughter, and hilarity. Altogether, for role enactment to succeed, the substitution has to be credible as is the case when a player pretends that a stick is his horse or that a shoebox is an imaginary airplane. In these and similar roles, the child does not defy the laws of gravity, and maintains throughout the game the distinction between reality and fantasy. It is in the realm of pretense play that the preschooler develops the ability to represent absent realities and displays a remarkable flexibility of thought, namely, the ability to operate simultaneously on two contrasting levels without confusing the two.

Between the ages of 3 and 4 make-believe play emerges as a major source of pleasure for the preschooler, among others, pleasure in inventing distortions, funny names for the partner, pseudo-insulting ones like "poophead" and other violations of ordinary reality. Sometimes a play episode begins with "what shall I be today?" as the preschooler initiates, alone or with a partner, at first simple themes and later more extended ones beginning with variations on the child's daily experiences: home, the parents, school, a visit to the doctor, a birthday party, a wedding, and other similar themes. Home and the family are of course common themes, with the dominant partner usually choosing the role of parent and relegating the complementary role of the baby or the pet to others. The parent is doing chores such as cooking, looking after the baby, but also going to work, and the dialogues are variations of snips of conversation overheard at home. Other topics involve shopping, going to the supermarket, bringing the sick child to the doctor, and more adventurous themes of firefighters, hunting, capturing criminals and locking them up in the prison. Other sources derive from fairytales or television programs as the following example illustrates. On a visit to a nursery school I observed a 3-year-old boy who, craving privacy, was playing by himself in a corner of the room, engaged in what appeared to be a strange game. He was rapidly and noisily opening and closing a number of drawers, gesticulating and talking loudly. When I came closer he seemed somewhat embarrassed and confided that he was killing the wolf, apparently enacting the role of the hunter in *Red Riding Hood.*

By the age of 3, preschoolers can employ all the basic elements that constitute pretense play either in a solitary setting or with a partner. They can engage in lengthy play episodes either alone or with a companion if they can negotiate the theme and the role of its actors. When the topic is "private" two players may lower their voices when an adult approaches and then reduce it to a whisper, certainly an indication that pretense play, even at this age, can be very private, akin to sharing a secret or a confession of sorts. Overall, there has been notable progress in the ability to adopt a role: going beyond the earlier simple enactment on self to a role that is implied and not yet named, and now to the adoption of a well-defined role. Among the different roles preschoolers may be inclined to adopt is impersonation, the adoption of a new identity for the self. Imaginative children may invent a pretend identity for themselves by impersonating the attributes of another human or an animal, enacting the typical gestures, movements, and sounds of the adopted pretend self, and sustaining the impersonation over days.

To engage in a make-believe game the actors have to convey a message by facial expression and gestures, a message that says "this is pretense and we both know it" or rely on the common opening "let's pretend I am…and you are…" The partners establish a frame of pretense within which they develop an "as-if" scene, specify props, activities, and, above all, their roles. Role play is, of course, a social event that reflects their knowledge of social relations and of the conventions of communication which they reenact according to their understanding and individual inclination. Successful make-believe play involves negotiations about script, roles, and actions, and attention to the intonation of speech that is appropriate for the character, for example, a mom speaking to her baby in the high voice of "motherese" and a parent using the address "honey" or a similar expression borrowed from the adult world. To the extent that the theme and the basic script derives from common, mostly family-based events, even young 3-year-olds are quite competent in establishing the play frame that is essential for the development of their chosen roles and the accompanying dialogue.

The roles preschoolers tend to adopt include primary family members, important others often based on the occupation of familiar characters, fictional characters based on fairytales, TV, Disney books, games such as Pokémon and Power Rangers, and, in the case of children for whom the biblical stories are embedded in their culture and upbringing, David and Goliath themes. Age and experience affect the number of roles, type of actions and interactions that can be accommodated in one play episode, and individual differences among the players can be quite marked. When playing with a single partner, the coordination of two roles that are familiar and routinely evoked, for example, a mom and dad, a mom and a baby, a teacher and a child, can be enacted with proficiency and some degree of elaboration. When the two partners are of similar ages, not much instruction is called for and the initiating child is likely to adopt the preferred role although some kind of turn taking may well be negotiated. When there is an age discrepancy, the younger child usually plays a subordinate role and is repeatedly instructed in the way "a baby or even a daddy" speaks and behaves. It is quite striking to observe the ease with which roles are adopted, embellished, and adapted to the play theme, and the sophistication that underlies the pretense mode even at this age. The ease with which imagined events can be represented by a 3-year-old is nicely demonstrated in this scene observed on a playground where a boy placed himself on a "tunnel" that connects a slide and a ladder.

Boy: "I am relaxing, no one can come through. I locked the door."

Adult: "Can you give me the key to unlock this heavy door?"

Boy: [Extends his arm and offers the key.]

Adult: [Takes the pretend key, pretends to put it into an imaginary key slot and slowly turns the key two or three times.] "Now the door is open."

Boy: "Now give me back the key." [Extends his arm to recover the imaginary key.]

In this case, it is the child who initiates the pretense game with an adult partner. But even when a game is initiated by an adult, the preschooler tends to take charge and to elaborate on the theme in personal ways. In such a game, Alexandra, a 3-year-old, was told that a blanket was a deep river and asked whether she can swim. She replied: "I could swim in a pretend river…but let's pretend we are wild animals." When asked what "pretend" means she answered quite correctly: "Pretend means the thing is not it, it's really something else"—a reasonable response to a complicated question that even older children struggle to put into words. Finally, when asked "When we stop playing, who are you when we stop playing?" she answered without hesitation "We will be the same person we were when we came up [into this room]."

Echoes from the home front can be gleaned from this exchange between an adult and a preschooler:

Adult: "I'll make the cookie."

Tara: "No, I'll make the cookie."

Adult: "We can both make cookies."

Tara: "No, I'm the cooker."

Adult: "The cooker…"

Tara: "Yeah, you can be my friend but I'm going to cook. I'll cook the supper for us."

Adult: "OK. You think you could make me a cookie before supper because I'm so hungry, I haven't even had lunch yet?"

Tara: "No, I can't make cookies because they are for dessert. You'll have to wait till they are all done."

Make-believe play flourishes

The period from 4 to 7 years is often considered the highpoint of pretense play with children devoting much time to socio-dramatic play with their peers in preschool and kindergarten.[11] Socio-dramatic play is a joint venture of the participants who adopt the role of "actors" and develop their relationship as stipulated by the pretense scenario. Most Western child centers encourage some form of pretense play and children enthusiastically gather in special areas set aside for dress up that inspire pretense play themes, with the actors taking on diverse and complementary roles.

Although all the basic elements of pretense play have been in place for some time, certainly from the age of 3, a real blossoming occurs in the development of themes, both real and more fantasy oriented, the number of players that can be accommodated in the scenario, the ability to enact multiple roles and maintaining complementary relations with the play partners. Role play becomes more differentiated, for example, the mom's role is no longer limited to caring for the baby, she is also a wife to her husband, a sister to her brother, a neighbor, and perhaps a doctor to her patients. Role play calls for a wider set of social behaviors along with the appropriate style of conversation and dialogue. As previously noted, 3-year-olds are already quite competent at pretense play, but it is with the older children that we note a significant development in their ability to reflect on their roles, and to articulate in verbal terms that pretense is a form of thinking. Of course, these diverse social skills do not appear all at once, and pretense play benefits from practice and the support that can be provided by adults, especially the parent's active encouragement or at least its passive acceptance.

The evolving dramatic skills reflect the child's growing competence to represent social events and perspectives that differ from the ones commonly held by the child. Representing different identities requires a new degree of flexibility that enables the actor to juggle diverse roles and to avoid conflicts that would end the game. While such talents are not manifest overnight, they are exercised during this period and are likely to foster good social relations with peers. Children who are too timid to participate in the development of a pretense theme or are less experienced in the rules of entering such a game do not participate fully in the social life of the classroom.

While socio-dramatic play tends to become dominant in preschool and kindergarten classrooms where it is most often studied, it can also thrive at home with siblings and friends or in a solitary setting. Playing at home, almost anything can provoke a game of pretense which was the case for two sisters who, upon hearing their mother snoring during her afternoon rest, promptly enacted the story of Red Riding Hood and the snoring wolf surprised by the hunter. We also find 4-year-olds, who by choice are playing by themselves, create extensive storylines while animating their dolls, animals, puppets, and an assortment of miniature figures. I remember how my 4-year-old granddaughter Sariel would retreat to the family room, close the door behind her and for the next two to three hours create a fictional world she controlled, playing by herself with her extensive sets of animal and human figures, puppets, furniture, and farm equipment. While she also loved to play make-believe games with her best friend, she used to complain that Emma deviated too much from the way "real" characters are behaving which conflicted with her own preferences, an indication that even at this age individual differences in the style of pretense play can be significant.

Scripts and boundaries

At the heart of pretense play is the script or scenario that represents real or imagined life events and provides the framework that specifies roles, actions, and situational characteristics. At times the structure of a script can resemble a typical story schema that begins with an introduction or a setting of time and place, introduces one or more protagonists who face a problem and set themselves a goal, and finally the resolution of the problem that has been conquered and the goal attained. Of course, more complicated story schemas introduce additional complications and conflicts and their resolution is more dramatic. To the extent that children use a fairytale format and/or content for their pretense enactment, the story grammar model with which they are very familiar provides a structure for the development of the script, at times an abbreviated version that is perhaps less dramatic and does not require the resolution of a conflict. Indeed, scenarios differ significantly, depending on the individuality of the players and the motivating impulse for the script. (For a more detailed description of story grammar see Chapter 3.)

To enact a script, the play needs a narrator who informs the audience and the participants of the setting and the major events, for example "we are lost in the woods and are looking for berries..." The narrative voice is the voice of the dramatist who plays a major role in standing partially outside the pretense play-frame but also ready to enter as an actor who engages in conversation with the play partners. The narrative voice comments on the ongoing action and the direction the scenario takes the players, but it is not strictly limited and can take off in unanticipated directions. Another characteristic of socio-dramatic enactment is the voice of the stage manager who guides and corrects the action, especially the verbal part, stepping momentarily out of the pretense frame to provide instruction or correction. Frequently heard comments relate to the truth or reality value of the role, for example, "daddies don't speak like that" or "monsters don't cry but act scary," or "I'll tell you when it's morning and we get up." The different voices are often enacted by a single dominant player and reflect the level of complexity of socio-dramatic play.

The boundaries of the play-frame are of considerable interest and address the issue of how the role-playing child can enter the pretense frame and adhere to the fictional script while also being keenly aware of when to step out of the play-frame to direct the play and guide the actors as they develop the plot. In the past, some of the major writers about imaginary play assumed that the preschool child would face great difficulty when making the transition from pretense to reality, a finding that has not held up to systematic inquiry. It is quite remarkable how well the preschooler is able to step out of the make-believe play-frame to negotiate with the actors, to sketch and narrate the pretend theme, to act as stage manager and assign roles, and to interpret the ongoing action to the audience.

The concept of boundary is a convenient term for thinking about two ways of "being"—in the realm where imagination and fantasy rule—and the world of everyday reality. How children manage to navigate both worlds without confusing one with the other, to simultaneously maintain two separate systems has always intrigued students of child play. Research findings of the latter part of the

20th century revealed that infants are not born into a buzzing booming confusion but develop fairly early basic perceptual and cognitive abilities, and a rudimentary understanding of intentionality. The latter implies some understanding of mental events that somewhat later underpin the preschooler's ability to engage in make-believe play. Observations of pretense play reveal the extent to which preschoolers spontaneously interrupt their own make-believe actions in order to convey information to a partner, for example: "don't talk to me now, I can't hear you because I'm inside the store"; "pretend you don't know…but I know…"; "we play…then we…then it is nighttime…"; "you are still in the boat, you don't see me…"; "pretend you see a lot of fish." These kinds of spontaneously produced verbal boundary markers delineate what is inside and outside of the pretense frame; their frequency increases with age though even 3-year-olds already use them as they develop their pretense play scenario. Of course, if the theme is familiar to all players, it does not call for much stepping out of the play-frame. If the theme is less familiar, the dominant actor serves as the stage manager indicating what is happening and how it is proceeding, which is of course a sophisticated way of stepping out and narrating as well as guiding the development of the plot. Altogether, the verbal account of pretense actions increases with age and refers to such fantasy characters as Superman, Superwoman, Peter Pan, Teenage Mutant Ninja Turtles, and Spiderman. When playing with an adult companion who suggests the theme, children tend to transform themselves and the scenario, introducing their own original ideas into the game. The fluidity of the theme, the tendency to modify and transform actors and plot line increases with age, and 4- and 5-year-olds develop themes that can be quite imaginary and verge on daydreams. Regardless of the nature of the pretense enactment, the child who is involved in his or her make-believe play is constantly monitoring the relation between imagination and reality, and if and when the convergence between the two entails a risk to the reality factor, the game will be abruptly ended, a finding of special relevance to the emotional aspects of a plot, an issue to be taken up in the section about affect and cognition in pretense play.

Despite their competence as actors, the ability of the younger children to articulate their understanding is quite limited. However, by age 4 and 5 children most commonly stress that pretending is a form of thought and that thinking enables them to distinguish between what is real and merely make-believe. It is interesting that preschoolers who are quite certain about the fictional character of their pretense actions, of role play as an act of the imagination that has no bearing on their "real" self, are less sure about the nature of "magic." Unlike their affirmation that pretense play is not "real," many preschoolers and kindergarteners assign a reality status to "magic," that is, that some people or mythical creatures may have special powers to transform an object or person, a power the child lacks. For them magic implies a superior power that can truly transform the actor, and they contrast magic with pretense play which is not "real change." Magic and those who have magical powers can fulfill dreams and wishes and perhaps create true transformations. Of course, children have extensive experience with pretense play transformation and cancelation, mental events that they control and which they exercise at will, while magic seems to be the domain of special forces depicted in fairytales and children's story books, for example, in the Harry Potter novels and the culture at large that fosters a belief in prayer and miracles, and affirms the existence of Santa Claus and the Tooth Fairy. (For a more detailed account of magic see Chapter 3.)

So far I have talked about pretense play themes in a very general way without considering gender and its impact on the choice of the plot. Not surprisingly, we find that boys and girls tend to diverge in their favorite games. Girls prefer scenes from their domestic life that emphasize affiliation and nurturing while boys gravitate toward more fantasy and physical action oriented pretense scenarios that involve adventure, conflict, and warfare. Thus pretense play mirrors some of the gender-related differences one can observe on the playground and in the home when children play with their preferred toys. These differences reflect societal norms, more specifically the expectation of parents and teachers vis-à-vis boys and girls, but beyond the cultural aspect the differences also suggest a biological basis which is notable in infancy and reflects the higher activity level of male infants. Indeed, from infancy on, gender becomes a defining attribute of the child's sense of self and his or her place in the social fabric as reflected in many languages, for example, in the use of personal pronouns, articles, nouns, and the conjugation of verbs.

Given the social distinctions that characterize gender roles in the adult world, it is not surprising that the roles the child actors adopt in socio-dramatic play tend to be gender specific such that dads can do the cooking, and in a limited way can look after the baby, but the caretaking role is usually reserved for the mom and real role reversals are uncommon. Over the last few decades, as gender roles in the home life have become more diverse, dads can be more involved with housework than was the case before the gender revolution. Nevertheless, the mom is the person who relates to the babies and dads go to work. Role reversals are not spontaneously enacted and when encouraged by an adult tend to be resisted by the boys. Thus, dress up in the "girls' corner" is risky for boys who might lose status among their male peers, while the reverse is more acceptable to girls. In some girls the desire to change their gender may be quite intense, as in the case of Ruth who prayed to become a boy and until age 5 made clay penises for her girl dolls and thus transformed them into boys in her pretense play. During this game which she played repeatedly by herself, a deeply rooted desire was translated into a scene that fulfilled her wishes.

Imaginary playmates

Pretense play in the form of an imaginary playmate has long intrigued students of child play who report on its first appearance between the ages of 3 and 4 and at times even earlier, either in the form of a preferred soft toy animal or as an invisible friend. In the first case, the imaginary playmate is a visible and touchable named entity, inseparable from the child, one who shares his friend's everyday life, family routines, and other major events. Most commonly, the parents are aware of the importance of this friendship, encourage it, and participate in the fiction that is enacted over days, months, at times years. Many children expect that the named imaginary friend will participate in the daily routines such as sitting at the table for breakfast and dinner, accompany the child on trips and to school. The individual characteristics of an imaginary playmate can differ over time as the child abandons one friend and replaces him with a new one that meets current needs and wishes. The invention of an imaginary playmate is quite common among only children, children of a single parent family, and of families where there is a significant age spread between siblings.[12] The imaginary friend provides companionship and fills an important niche in the child's life, many hours of which are spent at home playing with the friend, engaging in conversation and pretend scenarios. These children have a rich imagination and seem well adjusted; having an imaginary playmate is not an indication that he or she is socially isolated or inept; quite the contrary seems to be the case, they are described as socially competent and likeable. Of course, the most well-known imaginary playmate is Winnie the Pooh, who played a central role in the life of his friend Christopher Robin and enriched the fantasy of its young and old readers.

Unlike the imaginary playmate who is physically present, some children invent an invisible imaginary friend who also participates in his or her everyday life, for whom a place is set at the table, and with whom the child consults and converses with the apparent approval and perhaps encouragement of the parent. This is a case of pure fantasy construction, independent of any visible physical props.

Imaginary friends appear in approximately the same proportion of boys and girls, with boys creating imaginary companions who tend to be heroic and more competent than the child himself, while girls create companions that need to be nurtured since they are less competent than the child who can assert her power and control. The individual characteristics of the imaginary companions vary widely but what they have in common is their freedom from the restrictions their friends face, and the leeway to express aggression without fear of direct retribution. In this guise they give voice to the child's feelings and also compensate for the limitations the child faces in his or her real life.

Between the ages of 4 and 5 there appears to be a high turnover of these friends with new ones supplanting older ones and by the time children reach the elementary school grades, ages 7 to 8, the imaginary companions are assumed to be gone. This would coincide with a change in parental attitudes which consider the fantasy friendships no longer age appropriate. However, many of these invisible friendships go underground and, no longer enacted publicly, they are enjoyed in the private realm of daydreaming, fantasy, or the creation of stories. Many such relationships continue till age 10 and some into adolescence and even adulthood, especially in the case of artistically inclined individuals. Among these children we also find the creation of paracosms, imaginary worlds inhabited by creatures that differ from our familiar universe and abide by the rules specified by its creator. These paracosms or alternative worlds can take a visible form in figures made of diverse materials, or they are developed on a mental plane, a fictional character engaged with as pure fantasy. These creations are often very private or shared with a single confidant. An example of such a paracosm, of the extensive creation of imaginary beings is presented by Brittney E.

Brittney E., inventor of an imaginary world

Brittney is a 16-year-old adolescent girl who has used pipe cleaners to model an elaborate collection of imaginary creatures that populate a universe composed of Earth, Water, Fire, Ice, and Wind. Her models include dragons as well as seemingly ordinary animals such as foxes, dolphins, horses, cats, snakes, bats, cranes, ravens, tigers, leopards, panthers, and wolves. All her creatures are exquisitely constructed and show evidence of originality and artistic talent (see Figure 25 on pp.87–90).

The characters that populate her universe represent both good and evil communities. The good community is led by a wise and noble leader, the white dragon king Dyaster who values equality and rules by consent. He is surrounded by many prominent characters, and his castle is home to a diverse group of animals privileged to live peacefully in the palace of the king. In contrast to the good king Dyaster stands the evil black dragon king Bones who is the keeper of dead souls. He resides in a black castle on top of a mountain and subjects his subordinates to a rigidly structured hierarchical rule. Not surprisingly, the relations among the members of his group are not friendly.

In order to create playmates for herself, Brittney started her pipe cleaner models at approximately age 7. In the beginning, the animals could neither speak nor think; they did not show signs of intelligence, but they could be played with. When she was 9 years old the dragons became action figures although they remained nameless. Somewhat later, she began to give them names although at first these were not yet definitive names. Over time she has created close to 100 figures and endowed each one with a distinctive name and identity, and shifted her representation to drawings with elaborate titles: "ethereal land of dreams," "twilight castle," and "plane of darkness." At bedtime she turns to her imaginary world, and for many hours engages mentally with her different characters: she visualizes a storyline and is simultaneously playwright, actor, and director as she develops the theme of building communities that sustain long-lasting relationships among their members. Although the characters have individual names, they are not yet fully developed personalities: "I have to play with them to discover their personalities as if I were meeting them for the first time."

In one of her written stories, in which she attempts to translate her imaginary games to paper, the oldest character is named Roxton, a red fox who serves as her alter ego. He is male, insecure about trying new things but strives to improve himself to gain confidence and to become more socially competent. Roxton is a loner who lives in an enchanted forest in the land of Lumatara, from whence he sets out to find a magic gem that will enhance his power to the benefit of the good of society and also bring him closer to King Dyaster and his community of friends.

While Brittney only indirectly identifies with Roxton and his aspirations, some children adopt imaginary identities for themselves, roles they inhabit and enact for a few hours or longer, as was the case for our artist Antonia who at various times transformed herself into a dog, pirate, princess, or Aladdin.

Affect and cognition

Pretend scenarios or narratives are of course more than scripts or story grammar; they involve the participants emotionally, and the satisfaction children experience during pretense play derives from the feelings they project onto the scenario. Most scenarios are ambiguously structured and can serve to project diverse and contradictory feelings for which the child does not have to take responsibility. This makes pretense so interesting and attractive to the players.

What are some of the emotions that 4- to 6-year-olds experience quite acutely and which may find some outlet in pretense play, dreams, and fantasy? Among the child's many sources of concern, the relationship to the parents and the siblings looms large. The parents are the source of intense feelings of love and anger, rivalry and desire to replace one of the parents, fear of abandonment and death, guilt and shame, rebellion and dependency. Of course, the dominant emotions are not only negative ones, there are also moments of feeling protected and safe, pride in accomplishments, beating the competition, growing up and being powerful. These and other emotions may find expression in various make-believe themes of home life, for example, transgressions that are punished and birthday parties that are celebrated, there may be hints of parental strife and getting lost in the supermarket. Aggression can be voiced in simulating car crashes and getting to the hospital, soldiers at war and capturing prisoners, monsters and witches. Pretense play has the great advantage of trying out scripts and feelings without any real-world consequences, and when the feelings are too threatening, the game is interrupted or ended. The fear that one may die and the finality of death is not yet understood by the young preschooler, but 4-year-olds can be quite frightened by the experience of death in the family, of a pet or a grandparent. The theme need not be unambiguously stated, but organizing a funeral for the parents who went on a trip and did not return opens avenues for the expression of multiple emotions: anger for being left, ambiguity in that they went on a trip, so there is no finality to their absence, a funeral which puts the child in charge of affairs, and thinking about finding another family to join. In this and similar cases, what is expressed symbolically is not fully owned, it does not reach reflective understanding which, of course, protects the child from feeling guilty and bad.

When the feelings that are aroused by the theme are too frightening, altering it can make it harmless or, if necessary, stepping out of pretense can end the episode. The following are examples of modifications of pretense play episodes or elements thereof that the playing child makes to reduce uncertainty or fear.

In one of our play scenarios, in which a child and an adult companion pretended to walk through a forest in which a monster lived, many children, especially the younger ones, the 3-year-olds, transformed the monster into a more friendly creature by stating: "it has no mouth," "we'll feed it some cheese," "it has no teeth," "it's a friendly monster," "it's a good monster," "it's a nice monster," all the while clutching the hand of the adult playmate or clinging to her skirt, while acknowledging that the monster is not real. These children were controlling their own emotional arousal and reducing it to a comfortable limit. A tolerable level of arousal enhances the pleasure in a game of pretense but crossing over into a scary fantasy elicits all the fears children experience: being devoured, deserted, attacked, hurt, lost. There are notable individual differences among the children with some enjoying the thrill of a pretend danger and enhancing it while others diminish it and even exit the game as the following examples illustrate.

Playing a game about a scary creature hiding in a box, 4-year-old Max "locked" the box so that the monster wouldn't get out. He seemed highly involved in the pretense episode and fearful as he held on to the door of the box. After the game which he played with his adult partner ended, he crept up to the box, opened it, looked inside and exclaimed: "It's just a little beast." Next, he lifted the invisible creature out of the box, put it into a play oven and destroyed it.

In a pretense play episode about a fishing trip, a 4-year-old boy and his adult companion climbed with their fishing gear into a big box that served as their pretend boat. Sam developed the theme of a giant hiding in the ocean and the following interaction ensued with Sam whispering:

> **Sam:** "Maybe some big giant is out there and he will rip the boat apart?"
>
> **Adult:** "You mean we have to hide so he can't see us?"
>
> **Sam:** [Standing up in the boat.] "It's not scary…" [Crouches in the boat, hiding.]
>
> **Adult:** "We have to hide again?"
>
> **Sam:** "Yea, but nobody is coming."
>
> **Adult:** "Just in case…?"
>
> **Sam:** "I don't want my turn anymore…I don't want to be in the boat. I was having a dream."

In some children the fear of a scary image may be so pronounced that it precludes even the beginning of a frightening play episode as in the case of 4-year-old Evie who is intensely afraid of masks and of scary TV programs. It's not a case of confusing reality and fantasy as her explanation reveals: "The picture gets into my brain, and when I close my eyes it comes back! Also in my dreams." As her statement indicates, there is a distinct difference between what the child knows to be real and the emotional arousal that can be very disturbing. The emotional experience is very real, it is not merely enacted but temporarily "lived." Children understand that a pretend frame of mind on a scary theme causes anxiety even if it is not "real," and a fear-evoking object or thought needs to be expunged, canceled, or diminished. Thus, it is not a question of confusing fantasy and reality, but dealing with the emotions that accompany thoughts and images. Their emotional responses to fear-evoking thoughts are not unlike the thoughts of an adult who, alone at night in his or her bed, hears suspicious noises (perhaps as the heating system comes on) and wonders whether someone is hiding underneath the bed, a thought that will keep the person awake.

For most preschoolers there is a gap in their ability to articulate their knowledge that pretense is not real, that is in their ability to provide a conceptually formulated verbal explanation of pretense. While all state that pretense is not real even if they are scared, and that it is in your mind, brain, or head, the explanations range widely. After playing a game that instructed children to imagine a monster or a bunny in a box, we asked them the following question: "If you pretend very hard that there is a monster (alternatively, a bunny) inside this box, how do you know if it is for real or for pretend?" The answers ranged as follows:

- "People just like to make up monsters. My mom told me there is no such thing as monsters. Let's play again and you growl and pretend you are a monster."

- "It's not real because bunnies are not in boxes."

- "The box is empty! I know because my dad told me. My dad is a hunter, he has a rifle and he shoots bears and he eats them."

- "It's real, a bear! Another bear is in that box! He is five. Let's hide."

- "It's not in there because there's not tigers in this country, only in the jungle."

- "We were just playing some game and nothing flew in here that I know of."

- "Because I didn't see anything real when I looked."

For most children the answers indicate an intuitive kind of knowledge, not yet consistently or logically ordered. However, some of the answers reflect an implicit knowledge of a logical order: "there was nothing in there when I looked and nothing flew in," so it must be empty.

This surprising ability of preschoolers to maintain a dual orientation toward the reality-pretend status of make-believe play suggests a precocious understanding of pretense as a mental activity, of the child who perceives himself as a thinker. In make-believe play the preschooler adopts a fictional identity, transforms objects according to the needs of the theme while maintaining his or her own real and enduring identity. The thought processes which underpin this form of behavior are quite flexible, an ability to move from one mental state to another and back without confusing the two states. Piaget termed this mental process "reversibility," the ability to remember the original state of a perceived event, to take note of the kinds of transformations that have been performed, and to deduce whether the changed appearance affects the matter, whether quantity, number, weight, or volume of an item. In a series of classical demonstrations of so-called conservation tasks, Piaget presented children with two beakers of colored water or two identical balls of clay and established that the amount in both displays is the same. Next, the water in one of the beakers is transferred to another, thinner and taller glass, or the clay in one of the balls is rolled out into a thin and long sausage-type. The child is asked whether the amount of water or clay is the same in the transformed item as in the original one. Under these conditions, preschoolers fail the task and declare that the tall and thin beaker has more water (since the water level has risen) and that the long snake-like clay has more matter. Between the ages of 5 to 7 children begin to discount the importance of the transformation and to state that the amount in both displays is the same since (a) nothing has been added or subtracted, (b) you can always return the water (clay) to the original beaker (round shape) to demonstrate that they are the same and that nothing has been added/subtracted, (c) compensation, the child points out that what is gained in one dimension (height of water level in the column; length of the clay snake) is lost in the other. The ability to reason about the perceived transformation is a mark of the reversibility of thought, of a growing mental maturity typical of what Piaget termed *concrete operational reasoning*.[13]

Since pretense play seems to be based on a similar form of mental reversibility that underlies the transformation of the identity of the child, the play objects, and the partners while simultaneously retaining the knowledge of the original and enduring identity, we engaged 4-year-olds in a series of pretense play themes, followed by questions about their pretense identity during the game and upon its ending. Children were asked what they were before we started to play, during the play, and after the game is over, and of course their answers were clear cut and coherent. The questions may have called attention to the mental processes they were engaged in, and lo and behold, although on a pretest all the children were non-conservers and failed the classical conservation tests, after the play sessions ended a significant number of the children gave genuine conserving responses although they had not been trained on these tasks. These findings provide evidence for the cognitive significance of pretense play which fosters abstract forms of reasoning not yet seen in other cognitive tasks. Thus, socio-dramatic play which goes beyond the concrete, perception-dominated present promotes a complex set of problem-solving skills such as understanding the intentions of others and the different perspectives of other minds, thought processes that are activated and exercised in a manner that is only later applied to other domains.

The socio-cultural milieu

I have stressed the universality of pretense play and sketched, in broad outlines, its development in a child-oriented environment that is supportive of this form of imaginative action. The emergence of pretense play as a typically human ability calls for an inquiry into its evolutionary antecedents in the animal world, especially among our closest kin, the non-human primates, and the role of culture in the expression of pretense play in different communities.

Anecdotal accounts of ethologists describe behaviors that strongly suggest elements of pretense such as a dog growling at his play object while also wagging his tail, indicating a friendly mood. Of special interest are the observations of the anthropologist Gregory Bateson who called attention to forms of play behavior seen among animals that signal a message "this is play," which seems especially relevant in juvenile monkeys and apes, in captivity as well as in the wild. Engaged in play fighting they put on a "play face" that contradicts the mimicked aggression and conveys via their truncated and exaggerated movements, facial expression, and vocalization that they do not intend to inflict harm. Whether this form of behavior can be classified as true pretense is questionable, but its distinction between real aggressive behavior with its attendant serious consequences for the antagonists and a playful mimicry provides an interesting analogy for the make-believe play of children.

Intensive studies conducted over many decades of some of the great apes who were reared in captivity, in close contact with their human caregivers and trained in sign language, report behaviors that are akin to children's pretense play. Most commonly seen is mimicry of the animal's own activities such as pretend eating and feeding and, somewhat less frequently, behaviors based on the actions of others, actions that their trainers modeled for them. The repetition of the animal's own actions on self and other objects is a form of ritualization where imitation becomes pretense, albeit of a simple form, reminiscent of 2-year-old children. From an evolutionary perspective these findings suggest shared origins of intentional and mind-mediated behaviors. However, despite the superficial similarity between the pretense play behavior of non-human primates and that of the human child, the differences in their developmental trajectory are striking, especially when we consider the richness, originality, and complexity of make-believe play of the 4- and 5-year olds.

So far, our review of the evolution of pretense play suggests that it unfolds best where play space as well as time are made available for playful interactions with a supportive adult. This seems to be the case in the United States, Europe, Australia, and Japan where mothers or alternative caretakers encourage infant, toddler, and preschool games of pretense.

Where social class, cultural, and economic conditions are vastly different, the incidence and form of pretense play will reflect the distinct lifestyles and values of the parents. Thus, for example the Inuit, a semi-nomadic hunting community from the East Canadian Arctic, employ a ritualized form of verbal pretense play that introduces the young preschooler to the value system, the norms, rules, ethics of the family. The playful teasing and affectionate interaction initiated by the mother is part of an elaborate process of socialization, teaching about the environment and how to cope with it, while all the while stressing the pretend nature of the verbal exchange. In other communities, where children as young as 4 and 5 years are expected to participate in the work that sustains the family, spontaneous engagement in pretense play with age mates is likely to be restricted. Religious beliefs and values may also play a role as, for example, in the families of the old order of Mennonites who disapprove of make-believe play which, in their view, is akin to deception, a position that is similar to that of the Mayans of the Yucatan in Mexico who view pretense play with suspicion. When not involved in work-related assignments, 3- to 5-year-old Mayan children play in their compounds, mostly games with rules and motor games, while older children, between the ages of 6 to 8, invent some forms of pretense play that is modeled on the familiar adult activities. Adult models that predict future roles and competencies rather than fantasy underpin this form of pretense play. A community's lack of support for imaginative play seems also to be the rule in Kenya, in India, and many countries in the Middle East, among them the Sinai Bedouins. In the latter case many parents seem to view pretense play as wasteful, not useful for the tasks the child will fulfill as a grownup. Despite the absence of adult support, in general children tend to create for themselves some form of pretense play; for example, the !kung children of the Kalahari Desert in West Africa play with sticks and pebbles in pretending to go on a hunt or herd cattle, South American Indian children create mud houses for their games, and youngsters of the Himba tribe in Namibia and the Tallensi of Northern Ghana model small clay figures of animals and humans that represent dominant themes in their lives.

Among students of children's play there seems to be considerable agreement that maternal playful interaction with the infant is a precursor of later evolving symbolic play, and that societies where such interactions are limited show a paucity of make-believe. In a society that values innovation and creativity pretense play seems well suited to roles and themes that are beyond the bounds of the child's everyday reality, that involve fantasy and improbable scenarios, and in the process enhance verbalization and foster some forms of abstract thought. Where the emphasis is on continuity, sameness, and the preservation of the status quo, pretense play might not find much support.

Play therapy

The previous sections highlighted major trends in imaginative play and pointed to its beneficial effects on children's social, cognitive, and emotional development. The child who is able to create and recreate real or imagined scripts can give expression to often puzzling, confusing or conflicting thoughts and feelings and in this process gain some mastery over distressing impulses. Above all, make-believe play places the actor in an active stance, reordering events and determining the outcome, even if only temporarily so. In play children come to know what it is they would like to do, what roles to select for themselves and their playmates. Given the opportunity, children select stories and roles that are personally very meaningful to them as Vivian Paley,[14] a highly gifted preschool and kindergarten teacher, has documented. The stories express the many worries of the young, fear of abandonment, of getting lost, of being bad and sad, of being an outsider, of changing into a powerful animal such as a lion or alligator or a mother tending to her babies. In her classroom, each child has the opportunity to tell the teacher, and of course the classmates, a story that is first recorded and then enacted by the players the story teller has selected. Through their stories that characterize each one of the tellers, children come to know each other and to discover themselves. In addition to the intense enjoyment children experience when their theme is acknowledged and enacted, they learn to organize their thoughts and expand their vocabulary. This format helps individual children to adapt to their new school environment and to cope with the many demands that it poses. It creates a bond between the children and fosters friendship and a sense of community.

In the case of a more troubled child, a child who has experienced a significant loss either through the divorce of the parents, death, abuse, or other forms of trauma, psychotherapy might be indicated and play therapy is usually a component, even a major one. Child psychotherapy dates back to the beginnings of psychoanalysis as a therapeutic technique first developed by Sigmund Freud who reported on a little boy, Hans, who had developed an acute phobia about leaving his house and being bitten by horses. Following this early report, psychotherapists began to focus on symbolic or make-believe play as a primary language for the expression of young children's emotional concerns, of worries and conflicts that might be age and stage specific but also the result of traumatic experiences beyond the scope of the child's ability to cope. The influential writings of Virginia Axline[15] on play therapy, especially her dramatic account of a severely disturbed 5-year-old boy described in *Dibs in Search of Self* and of the productive changes Dibs could make in his relationship to himself and his parents, called attention to her method of non-directive play therapy. Axline's emphasis is on facilitating the growth potential of the child in an atmosphere of acceptance, empathy, and affirmation of the child's right, reason, as well as autonomy to direct his actions during the play therapy sessions, and eventually beyond the session to his home life as well.

There are diverse approaches to psychotherapy with children and to play therapy as one vital component, but all of them have in common respect and empathy for the child and support for what, at the beginning of therapy, are often feeble attempts to create a play scenario that can express some of his or her concerns. The play therapist provides miniaturized items that mimic common objects such as male, female, and baby toy dolls, a doll house, cars, ambulance, etc. An abundance of paper, crayons, magic markers, paints and brushes is also available. During the session, the therapist follows the child's lead, responding to his or her actions and, depending on the therapeutic philosophy, expands on the child's comments, raises questions, rephrases, and/or interprets the player's actions. It is assumed that in the safe environment of the playroom and with the support of the therapist the child will be able to express some of the conflicting thoughts and feelings, develop a better sense of self and the ability to cope with the stresses of his or her environment.

The school-age child and beyond

The high season of make-believe play has come to an end, at least in the very open and public form we have come to know it among preschool children. A question of great interest is its fate—does this use of the imagination simply fade away to be replaced by new interests, for example, games with rules that become popular and begin to dominate interactions among peers in and out of school? Piaget, the great observer of children, was of the opinion that with the growth of logical thinking the elementary school child distances himself from the earlier subjective and unrealistic world of make-believe that provided short-term emotional satisfaction to the younger and more powerless self. In the early school grades the child encounters a different social world where rules, reason, and arguments play an increasingly important role in the regulation of social relations. Among the games children now favor are checkers, candy-land, monopoly, clue, card games, and chess, and of course the popular computer and video games that conquer the market, and the outdoor games of rule-governed team sports.

However, along with the new-found interest in games that specify the moves that are permissible and which all players have to abide by, make-believe games continue to entice some youngsters on the playground or in their backyard to enact their favorite themes. In the case of some highly motivated children such role play becomes their favorite activity, a striking example of which are the Brontë siblings, whose preferred pastime was to write and enact imaginative plots. Not surprisingly, the four siblings became writers in adulthood. In general, make-believe play tends to go underground, pursued as private entertainment, for example, in the case of the imaginary playmates who continue their friendship with many youngsters although their parents are no longer aware of their existence. In some cases the friendship with an imaginary companion may continue throughout the childhood years. Children like Brittney continue to create a whole world of imaginary beings, with stories that are only known to her and that are rarely shared with others. But beyond imaginary playmates, the school years, especially the middle and high-school years, offer opportunities for the writing, directing, and performing of plays, the reading of novels and the writing of poetry, which might be seen as an extension of the previous love affair with imaginative play. Perhaps, the tendency to talk to oneself, to engage in some form of monologue or dialogue as a commentary on ongoing thoughts and desires, which appears in the middle childhood years and flourishes during adolescence, continues the earlier habits of role play on an inner plane. One can perceive a thread that runs from childhood pretense play through adolescence to adulthood, with make-believe play as one of the sources that allow the imagination to flourish.

3

Between Fantasy and Fiction

The previous chapters highlighted the child's ability to symbolically evoke and represent an image or scene, which is at the heart of the creative endeavors of both child art and make-believe play. As we have seen, child art does not aim to produce a copy of reality and its appeal lies in its invention of forms and colors that meet the young artist's intuitive rules of likeness and aesthetics. In make-believe play as in child art, the ability to represent underpins the mental transformation of the self, the partner, and varied objects, changes in identity that form the core of a script to be enacted, if only for an audience of one. This ability to imagine and represent enables even the young child to go, temporarily, beyond the here-and-now and to enter the realm of the possible, mental activities that are shot through with emotion. Imagination, of course, also extends beyond these two domains, and we will explore its expression in dreams and daydreams, storytelling, fairytales, and magic.

Dreams

Dreams, the conscious though involuntary experiences that occur during sleep, have always presented somewhat of a puzzle. Where do they come from, what is their meaning, do they carry a message? In many cultures, dreams are taken very seriously; they are consulted before major decisions are taken and can be seen as prophetic, for example, in the biblical story of Joseph, whose dream interpretation freed him from prison and made him a valued advisor to Pharaoh, the ruler of Egypt.

A breakthrough in understanding the neurophysiology of dreaming occurred in the middle of the last century when Dement and Kleitman discovered that sleep is composed of different stages, one of which is accompanied by Rapid Eye Movements (REM) during which dreaming occurs. Measures on an electroencephalograph (EEG) revealed brain waves that distinguish between sleep and waking; in deep sleep the brain waves are slow, large, and regular in contrast to the more rapid and irregular brain waves when we are awake and alert. The sleeper cycles through four stages of sleep during which sleep progressively deepens: stage 1 is brief, followed by stage 2 during which sleep deepens, increasingly so during stages 3 and 4 which are accompanied by large, slow, and rhythmic brain waves. This cycle is then repeated, ascending from deep-deep sleep to stages 3 and 2, to be followed by a REM stage with increased autonomic activity that is marked by a quickening of the pulse, elevated blood pressure, an increase in respiration which becomes more irregular and is accompanied by sexual arousal. The brain waves during the REM stage resemble those of the normal waking state. This cycle of REM and non-REM is repeated four to five times during the night, with an average of 90 minutes of REM sleep and dreaming.

Children's dreams

As most parents know from their experience, children often wake up seemingly disturbed by a dream and in need of comfort and reassurance. When do children experience their first dreams and what sense can they make of this vivid experience that vanishes when they wake up? It has been a topic of great interest since it deals with the child's ability to distinguish between mental and physical events, between the perception of a physically present object and the more ephemeral thoughts about real and imagined ones, including the reality status of dreams.

The most comprehensive study on the incidence of dreaming in childhood has been undertaken by David Foulkes[16] who adapted a laboratory method, originally developed to record the sleep cycles and reports of dreaming of adults, to children. In a study based on a longitudinal design, 3- to 5-year-olds and 9- to 11-year-olds were seen over a period of five years; in a second cross-sectional study, 5- to 8-years-olds were seen in a single year, on three non-consecutive nights. In both studies, the children came to a laboratory that included a pleasant-looking bedroom and, before going to sleep, seven small metal disks were attached to the face and scalp of the child to record brain waves and eye movements. Tiny wires ran from the disks to a terminal box on the head of the bed, and from there a cable transmitted the electrical signals to an electroencephalograph in the control room. As soon as the recording indicated a REM state, Foulkes would wake the child up and ask: "What were you dreaming just before I woke you up?" or in the case of a young child who seemed unfamiliar with the term *dreaming*: "What were you seeing, what was happening before I woke you up?"

His findings indicate a paucity of dreams for the 3- to 5-year-olds, with only 15 percent reporting a dream. The dreams were brief, with 13–14 words per report. Few mentioned a social interaction, and description of an active self-character was rare. Foulkes compares the reports to a slide show, watching a somewhat static event with little movement such as "I am asleep in a bathtub," "I am eating." Animals populate those early dreams; they may derive from story books or fairytales but they do not comprise a narrative. Two years later, animals still populate the dreams, but now the children report more locomotion and the number of words used to describe the dream increases. Altogether, events and actors are joined in novel ways that do not ordinarily belong together and gradually the narrative becomes more coherent.

Foulkes reports major changes in dreams between the ages of 5 to 9 years. Dreams become longer, more frequent, more dreamlike, more active, feelings are expressed and the self participates in the action. What is dreamt is not daytime behavior and is more in line with interpretation and evaluation of a scene. Themes of aggression increase, often in the form of criticism, and both boys and girls are likely to be victims of aggression, a recurrent theme throughout the childhood and adolescent years. Between ages 7 to 9, when awakened during a REM phase, 43 percent of children report a dream but also on dreaming during non-REM stages. Narrative length and complexity increase with age, the self is more often represented, and the incidence of animal figures decreases. The dream scenarios of the 11- to 13-year-olds are well managed and reflect the individuality of the dreamer.

For Foulkes, dreaming is by definition a conscious experience; it is the awareness of being in an imagined world in which things happen. He identifies three conditions for dreaming to occur: cortical and cognitive activation that involve physiological and psychological processes; occlusion of external stimulation; relinquishing voluntary self-control and ideation. The cortical and cognitive activation yield conscious ideation that dictates the dreamlike format. From these criteria it follows that dreaming, which is a form of thinking, is absent in infants and first appears at ages 2½ to 3 years. The early dreams with their static imagery are not very imaginative; from a narrative point of view they are rather restricted which reflects the less developed cognitive abilities of the young child. Foulkes thinks that parents predispose their children to report bizarre dreams, that the stories parents elicit when a child wakes up, afraid of the dark and of being alone, do not reflect the actual dream content which, upon wakening, is soon forgotten. The fears of the dark, of being abandoned, and other scary thoughts might lead to the confabulations parents tend to interpret as "dream reports." After age 7, the dreamer is a more active figure in the dream which reflects the growing mental maturity of the child, and from age 9 the dream form begins to resemble that of the adult. For Foulkes, there is an essential similarity between dreaming and waking thoughts, a cognitive activity that extends over a continuum.

Remembered dreams

Of course children's dreams have been noted long before REM sleep was discovered and psychologists, especially those interested in child development, date the earliest dreams to around age 2. Piaget[17] who was an astute observer of his own children's development, also recorded first instances of dreaming at ages 1 year 9 months and 2 years, respectively. Between the ages of 2 and 3 years the frequency of dreams increased which the child, upon awakening, related in relatively short sentences. The dreams were usually quite pleasant ones but also included events that worried the child, such as "I am afraid of the lady who is singing. She is singing very loud. She is scolding me." Another example of a somewhat scary dream comes from X, age 2 years 8 months, who woke up with a loud scream: "It was all dark, and I saw a lady over there (pointing to her bed). That's why I screamed." She explained that it was the horrid lady, who stood with her legs apart and played with her feces. Piaget comments that the indecent lady only did what X pretended to make her dolls or other fictional characters do. He notes that while the topic of defecation in make-believe and word-play can be fun and the preschooler may enjoy the thrill of experiencing some fear around jokes of "poop," in dreams these events cause anxiety. Piaget thinks that in their symbolic structure as well as content dreams are closely related to make-believe play and are a continuation of this form of play. When talking about their dreams, children rearrange the elements and thus create a story. However, dreams are not made-up, they are consciously experienced by the child, and their content might be seen as a continuation of pretense play. In dreaming the control which the playing child exercises over his or her pretense theme and actions is lacking, and scary dreams or nightmares become more common from the age of 3 years on.

In contrast to Foulkes who stresses the paucity of dreams before the age of 5 years, authors who report on remembered dreams, elicited shortly after the child wakes up or some time thereafter, note a much higher incidence of dreams and also significant individual differences, with verbally skilled children reporting longer dreams. Animals still dominate the dream content, but family members begin to make an appearance. The incidence of animals in a dream heralds the appearance of violent images, with wild beasts frightening the dreamer. In the dreams of older children animals become more tame, with pets and farm animals replacing the more threatening wild ones. Overall, children report having more bad dreams than pleasant ones, the dreamer being the victim, frustrated, scared, chased, attacked, injured, lost, dying, caught in a car crash, and paralyzed. There seems to be a bias toward memorable or frightening dreams. The good dreams focus on playing with friends, getting presents, being loved, having an adventure, or a good performance. Boys experience more aggression in their dreams, with gender differences also notable in the location of the dream, more indoors scenes in the case of girls and outdoor settings for boys. There is also a gender difference in the characters that appear in a dream with girls reporting an equal number of males and females and boys a preponderance of males.

After age 5 dream sequences become longer and comprise more than a single scene. By 7 to 9 they have become more organized with a corresponding increase in word length, frequency of dreaming, and the experience of emotion, a developmental progression that at 11 to 13 approximates the overall structure of adult dreams.

Nightmares

When adults are interviewed about their earliest dream experiences they tend to recall dreams from ages 3 to 12 years. The great majority recall vivid dreams from early childhood, with a preponderance of dreams that were anxiety provoking, and even nightmarish in a mixture of elements derived from fantasy and reality that convey threat, physical aggression, and powerlessness. The recurrent traumatic dreams of some adults begin in childhood; they are anxiety dreams where the dreamer is threatened, pursued by wild animals, burglars, or is caught in a storm. Although some of the nightmares children experience can be attributed to such highly stressful events as parental divorce, a fatal illness, the death of a parent, a kidnapping, or sexual abuse, nightmares are a common experience for a majority of 3- to 6-year-olds who dream of wild animals, ghosts, monsters, witches or other supernatural beings that pursue them with the intent to inflict harm. The frequency of nightmares begins to decline for school-age children, with some 7- and 8-year-olds reporting nightmares once a week, a few at ages 9 and 10, and rarely thereafter.

Nightmares occur during a REM episode, late in the night or early in the morning, and the dominant emotion is terror that causes the person to wake up, often with a scream. The frequency and intensity of nightmares for the 3- to 6-year-olds suggests that this period, with its remarkable growth of the imagination, of the ability to think about the intentions of others, about being good or bad, abandoned and afraid to die, is stressful for the child. Along with the physical growth of the child and the amazing command of language and speech come, on the home front, new parental demands for obedience, for control of aggression and sibling rivalry, and, in the preschool or daycare center, accommodation to its different set of rules. The transition from the protected years of infancy and toddlerhood, to the expanding world of social interaction and its demands for mastering impulse control, is highly stressful for the child. From this perspective, the nightmares are an indication of the insecurities of the younger children in a period of transition, and as children adapt to their new social environment and become competent elementary school children, the frequency of nightmares declines.

Making sense of dreams

How do children understand their dreams and what status do they assign the reality-unreality of their dreams? At a fairly early age, 3-year-olds admit that dreams are not real, but for some years to come preschoolers and many kindergarteners seem to think that the dream is happening in the room as visible pictures. Of course, it has to be dark in order to have a dream, the dreamer has to be in bed, events are happening in front of the child and can be seen with the eyes. Could another person also see the child's dream? If pressed, the answer may affirm that another person who sleeps in the same bed with the dreamer may see the same dream. If questioned about the source of the dream, where it comes from and where it is happening, children tend to emphasize external sources such as coming from the dark, from his bed, from outside the window, from the wind. Somewhat later, the tendency is to assume that the source of the dream is in the head, in thought, perhaps in the dreamer's voice, but the events are still happening in the room because you could not see it if it remained inside the head.

The contrast between understanding pretense play and dreaming is quite stark. In the first case the child controls all aspects of the plot, from its beginning to the end. He or she exerts conscious control over the episode. Unlike make-believe play, dreams are involuntary conscious events over which the dreamer, who is totally within the dream world, has no control. Although children reach fairly early an understanding that the dream is an illusion and not "really real," the ability to differentiate between the dreamer's thoughts and the immediacy of the dream experience is much more difficult to achieve. Indeed, even adults don't have a clear understanding of where dreams come from and what, if any, function they might serve. However, once children decide that the dream is not real, they next consider that it may have something to do with the head, with thoughts of the order "you have thought about something and now you dream about it; you saw a scary man, and you dream about him." The question of where the dream is happening is somewhat more difficult to sort out but, eventually, the proposition emerges that it is happening in the mind.

For Piaget this was a long drawn-out developmental process, with a final phase of understanding the immaterial nature of the dream reached by the age of 11 to 12. Indeed, in his early study of children's understanding of the nature of dreams, his questions were very probing: Why do we dream? Where do dreams come from? Does it come from us or from outside? How is the dream made? What do we dream with? When you are in bed—where is the dream? These questions might be seen to be suggestive, "leading" the child to answer more fancifully than he or she might be inclined to under other conditions. However, any extensive probing might involve ambiguity, pushing the child beyond his or her usual horizon when pressed to account for the perplexing phenomenon of dreaming: its origin, location, organ, and cause.

Piaget's findings on the rather slowly developing understanding of dreaming as a mental activity have been replicated in a number of different studies which indicate that around the age of 6 years children have acquired a basic understanding of the mental nature of dreaming. Dreaming is now understood as a form of thought, invisible, interior, and individual. However, in more recent times, when questions have been paired down and call for a mere yes/no answer, and the child is offered cues that differentiate between dreams, pictures, and real physical objects, 5-year-olds show a better understanding and tend to identify dreams as products of thought. Most likely, this is an incomplete and fairly fragile understanding which might not hold up under intensive questioning or under conditions that are emotionally arousing. While acknowledging the mental origin of dreams, they also assert that they can control the content of their dreams and have the power to dream about pleasant things. This view, namely, that you can control the content of your dream, declines after ages 8 to 9 and reaches an adult understanding by age 11.

Daydreaming or waking fantasy

Daydreaming, in contrast to the episodic nature of dream thought, is an aspect of an ongoing thought process. When our thoughts are not focused on a current event such as holding a conversation with a partner, solving a problem, surveying a scene before acting on it, or many of the daily activities that demand our attention and exact a price when it lags, we may become aware of an ongoing mental activity of undirected thoughts, of fleeting images, sounds, words and sentences in the form of an inner dialogue that make up our stream of consciousness. Thinking appears to be a continuous mental activity, whether or not we are consciously aware of it and monitoring it. Within this wider frame of mental activity we might distinguish between daydreams and free-floating associations, moments of reverie and a spontaneous flow of images and thoughts of which we become aware mostly before falling asleep. Daydreaming revolves around a special and recurrent theme, it is a waking fantasy focused on the self or an idealized person and his or her accomplishments. It is a mostly visually constructed fictional story over which the daydreamer assumes control as he or she creates a mostly pleasing scenario. Unlike sleep dreams, waking fantasy allows the daydreamer to compose an appealing or flattering image of the self or of an admired figure, and some intense daydreamers create elaborately designed new identities for the self and, in some cases, a privately constructed world or paracosmos. Daydreams are highly personal; they are an individual's creation and as such can also evoke images of failure, guilt, and shame.

We can get a glimpse of elaborate daydream creations in the detailed reports of Jerome Singer[18] and the notes of the writer Jack Kerouac. Jerome Singer, a distinguished psychology professor, invented in his childhood and adolescence several alternative identities for himself and his team of fantasy players. Most of the themes originated between the ages of 7 and 11 and were built on a "central fantasy figure," often a sports-related superstar and his baseball or football team. Another recurrent fantasy, fully developed during his adolescent years, centered on a character called "Singer the Composer" who was a gifted pianist and composer. This fantasy involved creating extensive notebooks in which the compositions were described and evaluated. Even in adulthood, to fight boredom or to facilitate falling asleep at night, Singer evokes some of these fantasy creations, especially games that feature his fully developed sports hero and his football team.

Another example of extensive daydream creations during the adolescent years, that continued to engage their creator as an adult, can be seen in Jack Kerouac's intense involvement with his imaginary baseball team which included preparing the statistics of the performers, composing newsletters, reporting on financial news and imaginary contract disputes.

What do we know about the earliest daydreams in childhood and their precursors, and how can it be studied? It appears that between the ages of 6 and 13 a gradual transition occurs between fantasy that was enacted in make-believe play and a progressive internalization of private imagery in the form of daydreaming. Anecdotal accounts suggest that such daydreams may already occur during the preschool years, they become prevalent during the middle childhood years and peak during adolescence, ages 14 to 17.

Of course it is easier to study make-believe play than daydreaming since we can observe the actual play behavior of children and, depending on the questions we have in mind, introduce some new elements into the play situation and record the outcome. The direct observational element is, of course, missing when we gather information about daydreaming and have to rely on a child's answers to questions that probe the experience and memory by asking "Can you tell me a daydream?" and follow it up with more detailed questions such as: Do you sometimes see pictures of things in your head during the day? Do the people and things that you picture in your head sometimes seem so real that you think you can almost see or hear them in front of you? Do you have a special daydream that you like to think about over and over? Do you sometimes daydream about running away from someone who is trying to catch you and punish you? When you are daydreaming do you think about being the winner in a game that you like to play? Are your daydreams about things and people that could never really happen like monsters or fairies or men from outer space? Do you sometimes have daydreams about hitting or hurting someone that you don't like? Do you sometimes think about something bad you did that nobody knows about but you? When you are daydreaming, do you think about how to make or build something or how to put together a real hard puzzle?

There are few systematic studies on children's daydreams but in one groundbreaking study an extensive set of such questions was given to first and third graders (ages 6 and 8).[19] The results showed that the younger children, the first graders, reported more childlike, fanciful daydreams and also more scary ones while the older children, the third graders, reported more aggressive themes. Quite predictably, boys scored higher on heroic-adventure fantasies than girls who reported more fanciful but also more scary and unpleasant themes. Individual differences were also marked and quite consistent over time, with children who scored high on the fanciful-intense daydreaming style experiencing pleasant, vivid, childlike dreams. Children whose active-intellectual or problem-solving daydreaming style focused on how things fit together, tended to create heroic scenarios that emphasize competition and winning. A third style, a dysphoric aggressive style of daydreaming, was noted, a style associated with predominantly unpleasant feelings. While individual differences continue to mark the daydreams of older children, with increasing age they seem able to make a more positive use of daydreaming and visual imagery, with a concurrent decrease in feelings of guilt and fear of failure.

In an extensive longitudinal study of 9- to 15-year-olds Inge Strauch and Sybille Lederbogen[20] collected home dreams and waking fantasies at three age levels: 9–11, 11–13, and 13–15. The results show that word length in daydreams remains constant over these years, with girls more articulate than boys. In terms of the gender of the characters, boys surrounded themselves predominantly with males, whereas girls had a more balanced distribution of males and females. People who appeared in the daydreams were mostly familiar figures, and when joint sex groups were evoked they also included the opposite sex. Daydreams of joint sex groups increase in frequency starting at ages 11 to 13.

Daydreams differed from night dreams in a number of ways, including the setting, content, and agency. The setting in daydreams was mostly of the familiar indoors type closely associated with everyday life, and unlike the more phantastic settings in night dreams. Differences in content were somewhat gender dependent, with representation of animals common in the dreams of 9- to 11-year-old girls, absent from their daydream fantasies. The daydreams of girls but not of boys included, at all ages, somewhat more bizarre elements. Physical aggression which is prominent in the dreams of boys was much reduced in their daydreams, but remained high for girls. Pro-social acts of friendliness in daydreams were significantly higher for girls than for boys. A striking difference between dreams and daydreams concerns the nature of agency, with children, both boys and girls, taking an active role in their daydreams, in both aggressive and friendly interactions, while in their dreams they tend to be victims of aggression and the recipients of friendly interaction. The authors interpret this polarity in terms of self-presentation as follows: in their dreams children represent themselves the way they think of themselves in everyday life, while in their waking fantasies they imagine themselves as they wish to be. Altogether, fantasy scenarios can serve an adaptive function for dealing with the resentments and frustrations of everyday life, diminishing the pain of loneliness, and compensating for social isolation (see Brittney's nighttime creation of her alternative world, pp.120–1).

What impact does TV have on children's daydreams? While there is no general answer without specifying type of programs and the extent of time devoted to the tube, some studies indicate that extensive viewing stimulates daydreaming but it also reduces creative imagination, and the impact of watching highly aggressive and violent programs increases the likelihood that physical aggression will be acted out.

Story telling

The telling of stories, a major source of entertainment, has ancient roots in the culture of preliterate people. People would gather and listen to the story teller who created and recreated tales, drawn from the collective memory of the past and of the ancestors, tales that fostered a communal bond among the listeners. Folk tales, performed in prose or sung in the form of a long poem, often accompanied by a musical instrument, were performed for a mostly adult audience. The singers recited heroic deeds from the remote past or ballads of a romantic nature drawn from their repertoire of songs.[21] The tradition of telling stories has, of course, not ended with the advent of widespread literacy, and is especially of relevance to young children who are read or told stories at home and at school.

Verbally told stories make special cognitive demands on both teller and listener who have to make sense of the story without the benefit of the physical props that support such related art forms as make-believe play or drama. As the story unfolds, the listener, alone and without visual supports, has to keep track of the characters and their travails over time and space. How do children develop their understanding of stories and eventually become competent tellers of stories? Of the myriad cognitive skills that underlie story telling, the most basic ones concern the ordering of a series of events both temporally and spatially, including cause and effect relations, the adoption of a viewpoint that suits the narrator, and attention to the different voices of the characters that comprise the theme. Of course, a good story teller who wants to hold the attention of a listener has to meet additional requirements that involve theme, gesture, rhythm, humor, intonation, vocabulary, and effective emotional arousal. Constructing a meaningful story makes great demands on the young story teller and we might get a better appreciation of the task if we contrast it with the make-believe play that preschoolers master at a fairly early age. As we have seen, pretense involves enacting a role, both verbally and in terms of the kinds of physical actions that represent a familiar situation. The model for such a pretense episode usually derives from real-life events and the players act in real space, with physically available objects and potential feedback from play partners. By contrast, the telling of a story is a purely mentalistic event of stringing together sentences that convey the unfolding storyline, of which the young story teller may not yet know all the elements he or she is going to include. Altogether, the invention and telling of a story is a much more demanding task than reporting the memory of a dream or a daydream.

Since story telling is a socio-cultural event, what are the models or story formats children are exposed to, and how do they develop an understanding of the fictional nature of stories as distinct from talking about their own experiences, for example, what happened today on the playground? In most literate societies story telling, often accompanied by pictures from a picture book, is common fare in preschool and kindergarten classes and it is also customary for parents to read to their children at bedtime. Of course, stories can vary widely and range from the classic fairytales to adventure stories, to the imaginary worlds of Winnie the Pooh, Dr. Seuss, Curious George, Alice in Wonderland, Peter Pan, Where the Wild Things Are, and the adventures of Madeline. Thus children are exposed to many different types of stories and over time they extract the rules that underpin story construction which makes it relatively easy to follow the development of a theme. However diverse the stories may be, they have a common grammatical structure that begins with "Once upon a time," which signals that the story happened in the past and that it is fiction. The stage is now set for a sketch of the major events of the story, its conflicts and resolution, and ends with a likely declaration of "This is the end."

In their efforts to understand the child's story construction and comprehension, psychologists have adapted some of the methods linguists developed for the analysis of folk tales to their study of children's stories. Inspired by these analyses, they propose that all fairytales and other types of children's stories are based on a set of common structural features, a story grammar that captures the regularity of a wide range of stories, and thus can also be used for an analysis of children's stories. Studies on comprehension and recall suggest that children gradually internalize the basic grammar which helps them organize the story as they hear it, store it, recall it, and also create their own.

Story grammars differ in the number of steps or levels of complexity that comprise a story, but in essence they are all following Aristotle's dictum that a narrative plot should have for its subject "a single action that is a complete whole in itself, with a beginning, a middle, and an end." A four-step grammar of what she terms a "primary narrative" has been proposed by Leondar[22] who considers plot construction at the core of a story. According to Leondar, the stories of young children are all plot and nothing else. The beginning sketches the setting and introduces the protagonist, next comes a disturbance of an existing state of affairs, which is followed by an action that reverses the misfortune, and an ending that restores the original status. Other more detailed story grammars include additional steps that represent an *internal* response, a record of the protagonist's reflection and feelings that indicate the teller's concern with psychological processes, a relatively late appearance in the stories of the older children.

Another useful form of story grammar, developed by the Marandas[23] who are folklorists, analyzes story complexity along four levels of increasing sophistication that reflect how the protagonist deals or fails to deal with adverse events:

Level 1: One power overwhelms another and there is no attempt at a response.

Level 2: The minor power attempts a response but fails.

Level 3: The minor power nullifies the original threat.

Level 4: The threat is nullified and the original circumstances are substantially transformed.

Of course, story grammar is but the skeletal structure that underlies a story, and in order to tell a tale children must have acquired some understanding of family relations, of good and bad, of right and wrong, of hero and villain, of strong and weak, of trust and mistrust, of loyalty and betrayal, the polarities that structure early experience and become the topic of many stories. In general, the different forms of story analysis have proved to be useful for an analysis of the stories of somewhat older children, from kindergarten and up, which means that we have to search for early forms of story construction and their antecedents before the stories become imprinted with the basic rules of story grammar.

Antecedents or early forms of story construction

Among the antecedents of the primary story plot format that comprises a beginning, middle, and an end we can identify at least two early sources: the monologues of toddlers and young preschoolers at bedtime, and stories that accompany make-believe play. Recordings from the crib, of toddlers' monologues before falling asleep reveal a stream of utterances composed of word play, memories of the day's events and plans for the morrow, repetitions, alliteration, rhythm, and permutation of words and sounds, a joy—almost a compulsion—in playing with words and sounds which is perhaps poetry-in-the-making, and foretells the verse stories of the 2- to 4-year-olds. Examples of such bedtime monologues come from Ruth Weir,[24] Anthony's mother, who recorded his nighttime musings before falling asleep. The following are fragments of his long nightly conversations with himself:

> Hi big Bob
> That's Bob [2×]
> Big Bob [3×]
> Little Bob
> Big and little
> Little Bobby
> Little Nancy
> Big Nancy
> Big Bob and Nancy and Bobby
> And Bob
> And two, three Bobbies
> Three Bobbies
> Four Bobbies
> Six
> Tell the night, Bobby
> Big Bob
> Big Bob not home
> Nancy and Wendy
> Wendy gave Anthony's
> On Nancy

Only Nancy could with the kitty
Mommy go sweep
Aw, Nancy again

        (Anthony, 2 years 6 months)

Don't touch Mommy Daddy's desk
I should
He says so [2×]
Daddy's desk and Mommy's desk
Don't take Daddy's glasses
Don't take it off
Don't take the glasses off
Daddy's wearing glasses
Daddy always
Dadada
Leave it
Daddy's glasses
Doggie, Mommy, cookie [2×]

        (Anthony, 2 years 6 months)

Such monologues are not uncommon among young preschoolers, but not all are verse-like, as Emily's extensive bedtime soliloquies, recorded by her parents between 21 and 36 months, illustrate. In Katherine Nelson's *Narratives from the Crib*[25] we learn about Emily's reviews of the day's events and previews of the next day, monologues that reflect her efforts to understand her world and to figure out puzzling events. Toward the end of the recording period her narratives also include fantasy elements akin to make-believe play. Nelson considers Emily's narratives as more suggestive of a novelist than a poet and she points to their function as problem-solving exercises, attempts to regulate her emotions, and desire to maintain contact with the parent who has abandoned her to her bedroom. An example of a fairly organized monologue that reads almost as a parody on parental demands for obedience shows how coherent the nighttime ruminations of this 2-year-old have become:

and we don't do it that much
but sometimes you go rinky-dinky all over the house
and do *that*
and go running away
and Stephen says I don't like it
why do you do *that* says Pooh-Bear
and my mom says you you look like a
and that's why you yeah
and that's why
why don't you go (walking with your bear)?
why why why why
why did you do *that* [5×]
why did you go flying about getting out of bed?
why do you do *that*?
I'm afraid you can't run around cause you are in bed
up and you wake up
why do you go running around when Stephen is
why do you do *that*?
I think you maybe wanna do *that*
but you can't
over and over you can't
I know you can't have matches match
you can't go with him in his (playpen)
one blanket two blankets bear blankets
why were you running around in Stephen's room
and the other room and another room?
children what are you doing?
why did you two do *that*?
you can't do *that*
you can't
and you can't go with Stephen
why do you go running and running running and anyplace?
I don't want you to go
don't want you to run outside

(Emily, 28 months and 21 days)

As Emily approaches her third birthday, the monologues peter out and one can assume that the thoughts which she previously expressed in her nightly narratives become interiorized as private conversations with the self.

We can also see how narrative emerges out of early symbolic play in which, at first, it is embedded. When 2-year-olds begin to tell stories while playing make-believe they lack the elementary units of plot structure and have not yet constructed a "boundary" around the fictional world they narrate. Thus, make-believe and narration are somewhat fused since the very young narrator lacks the distance of the story teller's perspective. If in the course of her pretense play with an adult partner one of the figures (for example, a girl-figure threatened by a replica lion) faces a problem, she is likely to intervene directly rather than narrate, from the girl's fictional perspective, a solution to the dilemma. For example, when the lion threatens the girl figure, the player simply removes the lion by putting him in a cage. A somewhat more advanced narrative solution might involve a hunter who shoots the lion, a solution that stays within the pretense play format. Indeed, when the 4-year-old narrator becomes a stage manager, her solutions respect the narrative-fictional bounds and pretense becomes increasingly language based. The child now begins to use gestures, pauses, and intonation to bring the story alive and the use of props declines. This development can be seen as an offshoot of the increasing complexity of sociodramatic play in which several partners adopt a role, and in the dramatic play staged with multiple replica figures whose voices are distinct. At this point in the evolution of pretense play the narrator has become an effective stage director able to monitor the different roles and perspectives of the figures. Indeed, by the age of 3 or 4, the child can adopt the triple roles of narrator, stage manager, and speaking for the figure-actor, and by age 5 she can construct a more autonomous fictional world in which the story aspires to a beginning, a middle, and an end.

Extensive collections of children's stories, collected by Pitcher and Prelinger[26] in the late 1950s and some decades later by Brian Sutton-Smith,[27] begin with the stories of 2-year-olds whose structure does not yet approach the primary narrative format identified by Leondar. Examples from the collection of Brain Sutton-Smith:

Frogs
they went in a house
they went in a park
they pushed on the people
the people got hurt
they got mad at the frogs.

(Clarence, 2 years 7 months)

The monkeys
they went up sky
they fall down
choochoo train in the sky
the train fall down in the sky
I fell down in the water
I got on my boat and my legs hurt
daddy fell down in the sky.

(Bill, 2 years 7 months)

There was a little bird named Bluejay
and he said "caw, caw"
a chair jumped over the truck
and a shoe stepped on a truck
and a mouse went on a train track
and that's the end.

(Alice, 2 years 8 months)

Batman got crashed in the fence
him fall down
him walk home
and then he went to bed
him have a good sleep
I finished.

(Cathy, 3 years 1 month)

Sutton-Smith points out that these stories lack a middle section, an
essential element of plot structure, and that there is very little sense of

time. The repetitions suggest a theme and variations, and indeed the same themes recur in the individual stories of the children recorded over many weeks and months. He considers these stories verse-like; they are told as lines and show some line-by-line size regularity. There are rhythmic elements and repetition of sounds, elements of alliteration and rhyme which characterize these early verse stories. They exhibit a poetic sensibility which declines with the advent of the primary narrative after age 4 or 5. Poems, however, continue to express some of the deepest feelings of the poet as seen in the following:

> I cough
> it goes up her back
> through her spine
> up her neck
> out her mouth
> to her head
> and she dies
>
> (M, 5 years)

Plot structure

Unlike the verse stories of the younger children, a bare bones plot structure is recognizable in the stories of the 5- and 6-year-olds who are asked "tell me a story that you have made up." The stories feature recurrent themes that are told over several weeks and even months as illustrated in the collection of Sutton-Smith, here told by two 5-year-olds, a boy and a girl. In both stories, there is a formal opening in the past tense, a brief description of the setting and an introduction of the characters, followed by a disruption or a disequilibrium, extreme hunger in the case of the dinosaur and loss or abandonment in the case of the duck. Both stories have a sort of formal ending, a punishment of the dinosaur for his gluttony and homelessness rectified in the case of the little duck.

The Fat Dinosaur

Once upon a time there was a great big dinosaur. He wanted a giant rabbit dinner. He found a tree. He never saw a tree before. He thought it was a rabbit. He tried to eat it but it was too hard. He looked and he found a real rabbit. He took it home, then he ate it. Someone knocked on the door then he opened it. He was still hungry. He saw an ant at the door and he ate it up. Then he ate a cow up. Then he found an elephant and he ate it up. Then when he was so fat he went to bed then he blew up. The end.

(Abe, age 5)

The Lost Duck

There was a father that had a little girl that's name was Sally. They had a duck pond. Once the little girl went out to the duck pond to see the ducks and she saw one little duck that was lost. And she took it home and she lived happily ever after.

(Agatha, age 5)

Between ages 4 and 10 children gradually develop an understanding of the conventions of story construction, from an event that might have happened in the past to a purely fictional event, which opens new perspectives on a world not as it is, but as it might be, a world of alternatives and possibilities rather than reality. In the beginning, the incidents are linked sentence by sentence, a kind of chaining of elements, elements that over time are organized or centered within an overall conception of the story which entails the ending within the initial situation. With the expansion of a fantasy world, the action moves away from the personal center, from close to home to distant times and places as the narrator moves the protagonist through space into new locales, although only those events are reported that are accessible to immediate observation. In the stories of the 6- to 10-year-olds we find some understanding of the intentions of the main characters, but only in the stories of the older children, ages 10 and above, does the story turn inward and show a concern with the motivation of the protagonist and the antagonist, with the inner life of the characters and their feelings. At this stage the stories become more complex with the protagonist making several attempts, not always successful, to achieve his or her goal. Further development in narrative competence can be seen in the stories of adolescents who not only report on the intentions of the protagonist but also interpret the motivations of the actors.

Content of stories

Themes of aggression play a large role in the stories of the younger children with references to broken and severed parts dominating the stories of 2- and 3-year-old boys, recurrent refrains of people and objects falling down, getting up and again falling down, with images of illness and ambulances at the center of the stories of 3- and 4-year-olds. There are references to daily routines of eating and going to bed, family dramas such as spankings for being naughty, and anger at the baby sibling. The stories of 5-year-old boys feature more impersonal threats such as car and plane crashes, storms and fires where violence is of a natural order. Boys seem to enjoy themes of violence and atrocities, with harsh punishments meted out for transgressions. Altogether, more misfortunes befall boys than girls and their catastrophes are larger.

Aggression also plays a significant role in girls' stories, with themes of injury and illness, of blood, stitches and needles, of crying but also of care, with more references to parents. Themes of aggression, death, and misfortune make up a large proportion of the stories of both boys and girls, with intensity of aggression characterizing the stories of boys, and sociability and crying more typical of girls. Consistent with the gender differences we have previously noted in the form in which aggression is expressed, animals in the tale of boys are large, ferocious, menacing, intent on biting, devouring, mutilating, and killing the victim, while girls populate their stories with domestic animals that have a friendly rather than a ferocious disposition. Between the ages of 3 to 8 years animals, both wild and domestic, are favorite themes, most likely stand-ins for the self and its conflicting emotions and troubles.

Differences in the narrative style of girls and boys extend to both form and content, with the stories of girls more coherently structured, depicting a more orderly world that neutralizes disruptive elements, while boys' stories are characterized by disruption and conflict. Girls structure their stories around stable social relationships with the family playing a central role, and fairytale characters of princes and princesses incorporated into themes of marriage and having babies. In contrast to the striving for stability in girls' stories, boys' loosely structured stories are characterized by action, excitement, rule breaking and delight in violence. The boys seem to be fascinated by disorder in contrast to the girls who strive to maintain or reestablish order.

When people appear in these early stories they remain for the most part unspecified as "mother," "child," or "friend"—they represent a generic character type which is also the case for such figures as fireman, policeman, doctor, and farmer, who are identified by their occupational roles. Females appear rarely in the stories of boys while girls also include such opposite sex characters as policeman or doctor. Fantasy figures are typecast as fairies, princesses, witches, ghosts, giants, warriors, and monsters, depending on time of year (Halloween), television programs, and current fairytales. For the older children, themes shift toward romance and science fiction and changes in plot development can be noted in the characters' treatment of conflict and disturbances of the status quo. While the younger children deal only passively with conflict, and their protagonist is easily overpowered by an antagonist and left helpless in a calamity, the older children address conflict using the more advanced coping strategies of the Maranda model by defeating the aggressor or outsmarting him, solutions which illustrate the impact of the cultural model of the hero tradition. The change from passively enduring adversity to active engagement also reflects the older child's striving for greater autonomy and a growing sense of self as an active and problem-solving agent whose courage, competence, and intelligence meet socio-cultural expectations. Overall, these changes in story construction and outcome are indicative of significant transformations in the cognitive, social, and emotional processes that define the middle and late childhood years.

Individual differences play a significant role in story content and style of construction with some children happily volunteering their stories to an interested adult, while others avoid such requests. Refusals may indicate a lack of interest or suggest a protective-defensive response on the part of the child who avoids entering into the realm of fantasy. Telling a story requires verbal competence and a delight in spinning a tale which animates many children between the ages 5 and

7 or 8, after which they show less readiness to volunteer their stories. The earlier pleasure in the telling of stories may later express itself in keeping a diary or the writing of stories and poems.

We have noted qualitative changes in the imaginative productions of the younger and older children, a playful imaginativeness that obeys its own rhythm and inner dynamics, unconstrained by rules of logic, order, and sequence in the case of the preschoolers, with older children showing a growing adherence to the constraints of time, space, order and coherence. The unconstrained spontaneity of the younger children has enthralled many a poet, and Kornei Chukovsky[28] a poet and celebrated writer of children's stories, who admires the linguistic genius of the 2- to 5-year-olds, bemoans the decline that sets in with the school-age child who fashions his thoughts to meet the reality of school and its demands for literal truth.

Creating stories and sharing them with others is a universally occurring phenomenon. It is a very effective way of conveying one's thoughts and feelings without risking rejection, nor having to take responsibility for its contents since, after all, it is only a story. Although the readiness to tell a story to a willing adult listener declines with age, the habit of constructing a tale may transfer to the personal and private level of our inner life where we keep an account of our past, present, and expectations of the future.

Fairytales

We have come to think of fairytales as a special genre of children's stories where such supernatural beings as fairies, witches, ogres, dragons, monsters, sorcerers and magicians dominate the scene. In this magical fictional world where kings, queens, and princes reside and animals can speak, the young protagonists struggle with adversity, often of an extreme kind that puts their lives at risk. But long before these fairytales became the domain of children they circulated among common people, mostly peasants living in villages across Europe and, far beyond, in the Near- and Far East. Among the early written collections of the 16th and 17th century, Charles Perrault's stories stand out for their adaptation to the tastes of the court of Louis XIV, which meant excising some of the coarser sexual references of the tales and adapting them to the cultivated sensibilities of his audience.

In Germany, the brothers Wilhelm and Jacob Grimm published their collection of folk or fairytales in 1812 as a study in German folklore, followed a decade later (1823) by a more restricted and edited version deemed suitable for children. Ever since their publication, generations of children have listened with rapture to their favorite fairytales, insisting on repeated hearings of the same tale. Fairytales maintain their preferred status for ages 6 to 10, but adults also report on the impact of tales that left an enduring impression. I can attest to such a long-lasting love of fairytales and a memory that endured over decades. When I was 15 years old, I spent some months with a family blessed with many children. As I went about the chores of housekeeping and food preparation, I would find time to tell the family's 4-year-old girl fairytales, mostly the one she requested time and again. She never forgot her love of the stories and the story teller, and contacted me many decades later.

What makes these stories so fascinating for children ages 4 to 8 or 9? In terms of their structure they follow the general outlines of the story episodes we previously encountered: an introductory setting that identifies the protagonist and the locale, followed by a calamity or challenge, struggles to cope with the perceived danger and attempts to find a solution to the dire situation, and most commonly (though not invariably) a happy ending. The characters are described in very general terms, for example, a beloved child, perhaps a prince or princess who becomes an orphan. In terms of time and place, the story is set in the past, in a far away land only minimally specified. However, the problems that confront its characters are intimately familiar to the child-listener who resonates to the emotions that the story evokes: loss of love and fear of abandonment, hunger, jealousy, envy, guilt, anger, greed, deceit, and betrayal. The tales focus on rivalry, neglect, suffering, and injustice, and at times on trickery as the young and weak outsmart the powerful. The design of the stories is simple, and the battle between good and evil appears clear cut, which makes it easy for children to identify with the protagonist. They experience the thrill of adventure and moments of fear but, as in all good fairytales, evil is vanquished in dramatic fashion. Above all, evil is externalized, embodied as it were by the antagonist, which can be reassuring to a child who struggles with feelings of being bad, jealous, greedy and other such human frailties.

Among many beloved fairytales, the opening is unthreatening with its reference to another, long-ago time, and an unknown place in a far away location. The central character of the story is a child, sometimes a newborn, described as beloved of its mother who, alas, shortly thereafter dies. After a while, the father remarries and the stepmother becomes the tormentor of the orphaned child as in the tale of *Cinderella*, determined to kill her as in the tales of *Snow White* and *The Juniper Tree*, or to abandon the children to death from starvation as in *Hansel and Gretel*. The sad themes of rivalry, jealousy, envy, humiliation, and injustice elicit strong emotions in the listener who is no stranger to feelings that call for retribution and the elimination of the evil stepmother-witch. In these and other similar stories, the father is describes being absent, weak, or unaware of the suffering his child is enduring. As the stories unfold rescue appears in the form of a fairy, a messenger-substitute for the good mother who continues to protect her child Cinderella; a good male figure who disobeys the order to kill Snow White, the kind dwarfs who host her, and a charmed prince who awakens her; or the clever intervention of one of the protagonists as in the case of Hansel and Gretel and the sister in *The Juniper Tree*. The stories end optimistically with evil eliminated, justice done, and the protagonists living happily ever after.

As told, the fairytale is both real and unreal, it tells of problems and conflicts that all children face, but it is unreal in its reference to the fictional-magical world of our fantasy life. The dynamics of family life are at once so familiar and so far away in the land of the fairytale, which poses a challenge for those who wish to interpret the content and its significance in the emotional life of the child. Among psychodynamically inclined psychologists, some have viewed the tales as mirroring a developmental journey toward maturity in the formation of the self, a task that involves impulse control and the integration of different aspects of the personality. Others have adopted a more explicitly psychoanalytic view of the centrality of the oedipal conflict in the emotional life of the child and the need to resolve it via sublimation of the primitive desires.

The Greek tale of Oedipus Rex recounts the tragedy of the son, abandoned in infancy, who unwittingly kills his father and marries his mother, and ends with the blinded son expelled from the kingdom. Of course there is a far cry between this intense drama and the yearnings of the young child who wants to marry the parent of the opposite sex. When you ask a 4-year-old boy whom he wants to marry, the answer most likely is "mom." When you inquire about dad and what is going to happen with him, the answer indicates that he is relegated or promoted to be the grandfather of their children. In the case of the girl, dad is the chosen marriage partner, especially if he is approachable and fun to be with. Beyond the innocence of these answers lie intense feelings for the parents, anguish at being excluded at night from their bedroom and the many times the parents pursue their own, adult entertainment. To be so close and yet excluded is a puzzling but also painful experience of many young children.

In his book *The Uses of Enchantment*, the psychoanalyst Bruno Bettelheim[29] considers the oedipal conflict to be at the heart of most if not all fairytales. The preschool child is torn between his love of the mother, in the case of the girl the love of the father, and the anger and hatred felt for the parent of the same sex. In order to posses the loved one, the competing parent has to be eliminated which, of course, causes intense confusion and anxiety, ambivalence and guilt feelings. The young child has no means of resolving the conflicting feelings of love for both parents and anger at the competing one; he is overtaken by anxiety that the all-powerful and knowing parent might take revenge and cause bodily harm, especially to his penis. In the classical Freudian version, the little girl has already discovered that she lacks a penis and fantasizes that her mother has robbed her of this valuable organ, even more reason to feel resentment toward her. The solution to this intense dilemma lies in a complex process of repression and renunciation of these libidinal desires along with accommodation of super-ego demands for conformity and social adaptation. The fairytale provides the emotionally conflicted child with the means to externalize the contradictory feelings about the parents, who are loved and resented, to whom he or she is deeply attached while nursing angry thoughts, for example, about the mother as evil stepmother and the father as monster or cannibalistic giant. In the fairytale the child's destructive wishes can be embodied in one figure while the idealized image can be maintained in yet another one. Moreover, the child can project all the hateful feelings, which are too scary to be acknowledged as emanating from the self, onto recognizable fairytale characters that are sketched in black and white terms.

It is Bettelheim's view that the stories speak on a symbolic level to the emotional turmoil and confusion of the preschool age child, and that they hold out the promise of an acceptable and satisfying solution. The assumption that the symbolism of the fairytales speaks to the unconscious of the child and helps it resolve the inner conflicts and move beyond them to a less stressful stage in his or her social and emotional development underpins Bettelheim's interpretation of all the fairytales. Some examples that illustrate the tenor of his arguments can be seen in the stories of *Hansel and Gretel, Little Red Riding Hood, Jack and the Beanstalk, Cinderella, Snow White,* and *Goldilocks and the Three Bears.* According to Bettelheim, the different fairytales appeal to the child at the different stages of his or her psycho-sexual development.

The tale of *Hansel and Gretel* deals with oral frustration and oral regression in the orgy of greedily demolishing the gingerbread house that ought to serve as their shelter. As the story unfolds, the two siblings cooperate in rescuing each other, they meet new challenges, develop initiatives and plan their return home. Their passage home over water signals a transition to a higher level of development; they have overcome their oral fixations, their immature oedipal dependence on the parents, and in the process they have undergone significant developmental changes that are of an internal nature. In Bettelheim's account, this is a story of growth from primitive regressive tendencies to an intelligent integration of the child's thoughts and feelings.

The tale of *Little Red Riding Hood* is interpreted as a story about a pubescent girl who has not yet resolved the oedipal attachments that linger on in her unconscious, and therefore make her vulnerable to seduction and premature sex. She does not heed the warning not to stray from her path to grandma's house and carelessly gives the wolf (a stand-in for the father figure and her erotic feelings for him) directions to her home, thus expressing an unconscious wish to eliminate the grandmother (a representation of the mother figure). In Bettelheim's view this marks a regression to oedipal longings and an immature way of handling her budding sexuality which is also expressed in the splitting of the father image into a ferocious animal and the hunter-rescuer. While the figure of the wolf represents the seducer, it also serves to externalize the badness the child feels for having ignored the parental admonitions and betrayed her trust. Her return from the wolf's stomach is seen as symbolic of her inner transformation. The story ends: "But Little Red Cap thought 'as long as you live, you won't run off the path into the woods all by yourself when mother has forbidden you to do so.'" According to Bettelheim, the child has an intuitive understanding of the meaning of this story and the need to overcome the oedipal desires that threaten her with chaos.

In *Jack and the Beanstalk*, the boy is forced to outgrow his oral dependency since the good cow Milkie White no longer produces milk. He is sent out into the world to sell the cow and bring home money to sustain the family (mother and son). Jack leaves with the cow and is persuaded to trade it for a magical object, a wondrous stick, a singing bee, and on his third trip, a handful of bean seeds. Upon his return, his mother berates him for his foolish acts to exchange a cow for seeds, and in her anger throws the seeds away and punishes Jack by sending him to bed without a meal. When Jack awakes, his room is darkened by a huge beanstalk that extends from the ground up to the sky. The story tells about Jack's adventure, climbing the beanstalk as if it were a giant ladder, his encounter with a cannibalistic ogre, his rescue by the benevolent wife of the ogre, his theft of the giant's treasures, a sack of gold on the first excursion, a hen that lays golden eggs on the second one, and on the third and most hazardous one—a golden harp. On the last and final trip, Jack barely makes his escape from the furious ogre who pursues him down the ladder, but Jack's decisive action of cutting the beanstalk rescues him and destroys the giant who falls to his death. In Bettelheim's interpretation, the beanstalk represents the phallic wishes of the oedipal child, to be masculine and also to be rid of the threatening father who wants to devour him. Once again, the oedipal conflict is externalized in two opposing figures, the evil ogre and his good wife. It is the story of a boy trying to outgrow oral dependency, to gain independence and achieve greatness. As the story ends Jack is ready to give up phallic and oedipal fantasies, the wondrous beanstalk has been cut down, and he now tries to live in reality. Bettelheim suggests that the acquisition of the golden harp stands for a higher level of development that values beauty and art.

Themes of aggression and of cruel punishments have been an integral part of most fairytales and many a parent has felt inclined to censor or minimize these parts of the story. Bettelheim takes issue with this form of "sanitizing" the story which speaks to the child's own needs for rewarding the good and punishing the evil doers; it is an integral part of the meaning of the story and its attraction. However, more serious questions have been raised about Bettelheim's contention that the symbolism of the fairytale and its deeper meaning is accessible to the preschool child, the 4- and 5-year-olds who struggle with their conflicting desires and emotions. It is a comforting thought that fairytales promise relief from the existential pressures of the child and that they hold out a map of the territory that needs to be traversed. The tales speak to the eternal fears and longings of childhood, of abandonment, humiliation, and how to outdo the siblings, gain riches and finding one's luck elsewhere, and on this level the story speaks for itself. But from a psychoanalytic perspective these are just surface characteristics and deeper oedipal conflicts underlie these tales.

So, how are we to understand the thesis that the symbolism of the tale relates to the child's unconscious when the latter, almost by definition, does not reach the child's awareness? The proposition that unconscious or preconscious thoughts are somehow accessible to the child, who can grasp the symbolic meaning of the tale, is difficult to validate empirically. There are, however, some studies[30] that suggest that children are aware of the dynamics that underlie their relationship to the parents and their conflict-ridden emotions. Exploring the effects of listening to a fairytale, 6- to 11-year-olds were exposed to one of three conditions: listening to the fairytale *The Juniper Tree* or *The Goose Girl*, viewing a popular film *Popeye Meets Sinbad*, or listening to an adventure story. The responses of the three groups were quite different. The children who had listened to the fairytale were silent, very subdued and self-absorbed which contrasted markedly with the behavior of the children in the other two groups who, following this interlude, were more socially interactive. The fairytales seemed to have touched the children's inner concerns and left them in a pensive mood. Findings from a more recent study of 6- to 12-year-olds also provide some support for a psychoanalytic interpretation of the fairytales *Little Red Riding Hood* and *Snow White*. [31] The stories elicited oedipal and aggressive feelings, as well as anxiety related to punishment for wrong doing, although it should be noted that the older children could articulate their feelings better than the younger ones.

Beyond the question of the meaning children derive from listening to fairytales lurks another one, namely, whether children can distinguish between realistic stories that tell about events that could happen in everyday life and fairytales where ordinary rules of causality are suspended. In a thoughtful study[32] that compared 3-, 4-, and 5-year-olds' responses to fairytales, realistic, and religious stories, children showed a surprising ability to differentiate between the different genres. All the children rejected the reality status of the fantastic tales, and the majority of 3- and 4-year-olds also maintained that the religious stories of miraculous events could not happen in reality. However the 5-year-olds differed from the younger children on the religious stories in asserting in greater numbers that the story could have happened in reality, that is to say that the characters presented had a historical reality. Not surprisingly, the children who asserted that the events portrayed in the religious stories could have happened came from families who were religiously inclined, and most of these 5-year-olds were enrolled in a religiously oriented daycare center. Overall, these preschoolers were quite skeptical about the reality status of the fictional characters, but the findings also indicate that with age children develop a growing appreciation that certain types of events and story characters might represent reality.

Magic

So far we have seen that preschoolers develop a fairly good understanding that make-believe differs from reality, dreams are a form of illusion, fairytales belong to a domain of fantasy, and that stories in general do not refer to characters acting in the real world. This account differs in several ways from Piaget's early writings that stressed the conceptual immaturity of the preschool child whose reasoning is marked by what he called an excessive form of assimilation, a tendency to distort the perception of reality in the direction of wish fulfillment and subjective feelings. His work on the child's conception of the world[33] emphasized that early in their development, children do not clearly distinguish between mental and physical events, that they experience most natural phenomena as governed by various forms of animism and magic, a world where wishes and intentions rule supreme. He inferred a widespread form of magical thinking that personifies the world and endows nature with the same spirit of intentions, wishes, and inclinations the child knows from his or her own experience. This form of pre-causal reasoning is gradually restrained as the school-age child's reasoning becomes more systematic, verbally articulate and logical, and intuitions are subjected to empirical verification.

This account seems at odds with much of our earlier discussions on preschoolers' ability to differentiate various forms of fantasy from reality, and it is especially surprising since some of Piaget's more interesting and perhaps poetic examples of animism come from 11–12-year-olds. Indeed, following his early publications, many studies challenged Piaget's emphasis on animism and magic as defining characteristics of the mental life of preschoolers, and strove to depict a more balanced view of their competencies. However, magical thinking does not altogether disappear with development; witness the widespread cultural images of Santa Claus and the Tooth Fairy, nighttime fears of witches, and in adulthood, belief in the supernatural powers of ghosts, spirits, angels, devils, the evil eye, and such bad omens as crossing paths with a black cat. Altogether, children live in a social world that often refers to puzzling effects as due to "magic" or magical tricks. If we adopt a dictionary definition of magic as "the art that purports to control or forecast natural events, effects, or forces by invoking the supernatural" and extend the definition to also include mental acts that have the power to affect a distant object, we might consider a number of propositions: (1) Following Piaget's analysis, children are by the nature of their immature thought processes prone to magical thinking; (2) Children are duped by adults who wish to sustain their own fond memory of the magic of childhood; (3) Humans, by their mental make-up, are prone to magical experiences that are never fully outgrown and continue to exert their influence in a shadowy land occupied by dreams and fantasies.

As a first step in our inquiry we ought to clarify what we mean when we think about magic and children. The proposition that unseen forces pull strings and rearrange cause and effect relations, the very idea of invisible forces that control some aspect of nature, humans included, is a fairly sophisticated conception of the world, and so is the belief that one's thoughts can produce external effects. Of course, the simple everyday reality of cause and effect has been mastered by the 2-year-old who takes objects apart, and sometimes also puts them together, picks up toys, winds them up rather than winking at them in the hope that they will obey his or her commandments without having to exert any physical effort. Toddlers are quite successful in employing their understanding of cause and effect in action but not yet in the domain of verbal logical reasoning. Indeed, when Piaget questioned preschoolers about the movement of the celestial bodies, the sun, moon, and stars, the answers suggested a belief in magic and animism, for example, the moon follows the child on his walk either because the child wishes/commands it (magic) or because the moon desires to do so on its own (animism). Responses to questions about dreams and where they come from, what makes the wind and the clouds move, the origins of rivers and lakes, all seemed to point to magical forms of reasoning regarding phenomena that are beyond the ability of the child to control, examine, or experiment with. The answers of the 3- to 5-year-olds were rather prosaic and difficult to characterize; however, the older children attributed consciousness to the celestial bodies and other phenomena of nature, with the most articulate examples coming from the older children, ages 11 to 12. Altogether, Piaget records a blossoming of animistic and magical attribution, a poetic vision that animates the images of nature which, from the age of 8 years on, begin to lose their physiognomic qualities. As nature is gradually devitalized the child withdraws its subjective projections and comes to regard nature in terms of indifferent, mechanical-causal relations. The young human begins to differentiate between her thoughts and feelings and the inanimate world; she develops an impersonal investigative attitude which will eventually enable her to exert control and mastery over nature. Prior to this dissociation, similar laws applied to the realm of life and nature, mind and matter, but with the "split" the child will have lost this early sense of unity with the world, and from now on, for better or for worse, will become relatively free from the bonds of magical thinking.

One can draw diverse conclusions from the examples offered by Piaget in *The Child's Conception of the World* which he published in 1929 concerning the methods of verbal inquiry, the age ranges, and the socio-cultural environment, but above all one is struck by the fact that the children were faced with imponderables, far away objects that can't be examined, manipulated or explored. Forced to offer their thoughts, and trying to make sense of them in the absence of relevant information, they drew upon their own experience with desires, intentions, and motivation which provided the basis for characterizing their thoughts in terms of magic and animism.

This view of the preschooler's magical reasoning and its extension to children throughout the elementary school grades has not gone untested and many studies have questioned the reality of these "magical years."[34] When faced with clear violations of cause-effect relations as in the case of a screen seemingly passing through a solid obstacle, 4-year-olds tend to be skeptical and look for "magical tricks" rather than accepting an explanation of magic. Even in the case of the moon illusion, the impression that the moon coordinates its movement with that of the child going for a walk at night was rejected by this preschooler: "the moon doesn't know about me, where I am, he has no face, cannot know" (Maya, 4 years 10 months). Thus, an important question revolves around the preschooler's use of the term *magic* and what meaning it may have in the different contexts in which it seems to apply.

Magic is quite explicitly introduced in the lives of 3- and 4-year-olds when fairytales begin to play a role, with parents reading such stories during bedtime and at other times as a form of entertainment. More significantly, perhaps, parents introduce their children to that magical figure, Santa Claus, who visits on the same night all the children of the world and brings them presents. Likewise, children become familiar with the Tooth Fairy who eagerly collects their baby teeth and compensates them for their loss with a valuable coin placed underneath their bed pillow. Of course, the adult world introduces the child also to other mythical figures, often benevolent creatures such as the Easter Bunny but, depending on cultural values, also threatening figures that are likely to punish the child for various misdeeds. Given society's introduction of magical figures into the mental life of children, what kind of magical beliefs does the preschooler entertain? Various studies suggest that while 2½-year-olds lack the concept of magic and do not use such terms, 4-year-olds refer to magic, especially when they don't have a ready-made explanation for puzzling events, and such appeals to magic peak around the age of 6. Note, however, that the word magic is applied selectively, and children tend to reserve magical explanations for events they consider impossible, that is, when their usual appeal to physical causal explanations fails, and the reference to the power of a magician or to magical tricks provides an alternative account. References to magic are not their usual default explanation, but when their efforts to provide physical causal explanations fail (for example, under special experimental conditions) they may have recourse to an alternative form of causal reasoning that applies only to special events. Of course, it is difficult to distinguish between a genuine belief in the magic of special causality, one that is limited to particular conditions, and conventional explanations that refer to magical events or tricks. However, in the realm of psychological causality, the belief that thoughts and wishes can have an effect on physical reality is a variant of magical thinking, one that is quite prevalent in the preschool years, and later in the form of prayer. Between the ages of 3 and 5–6, children consider wishing to be an act of magic and they seem to believe that the wish will come true. Remember the 4-year-old girl (Chapter 2, p.118) who wished to become a boy with a penis and ardently prayed for this change in her gender; by the age of 5–6 she knew that wishes and prayers did not help her, and that she had to resign herself to being a girl. In her case, this insight into the limits of wishing coincides with the conceptual development of gender permanence and constancy, the knowledge that gender is constant, independent of wishes, clothing, and behavior. While praying can be seen as a socially transmitted form of wishing, it seems to correspond to a basic human need, irrespective of age.

A naive as well as a sophisticated conception of natural laws is reassuring and makes the world understandable and predictable, an understanding that grows with age and education and eventually can be expressed verbally and mathematically. However, mental life is not restricted to these forms of reasoning, and belief in and fear of demons continue to populate the imagination of children and adults. The 5- or 6-year-old who is afraid of a witch when alone in bed at night may well explain during daytime that witches exist only in fairytales, but her fear is real and her imagination vivid. All kinds of evil forces can be imagined to invade the sleep and dream of the child unprotected in her bed which, paradoxically, parental magic might control. Some writers propose that alongside logical reasoning based on conceptions of physical causality there exists a parallel universe of a more primitive order where different rules apply. One might refer to physiognomic perception, an untutored and direct response to the expressive characteristics of the environment, for example, to dark and ominous-looking clouds that forebode ill, or a bright and sunny day that foretells pleasure and cheerfulness. When a series of unusual events happen for which no ordinary causal explanation is readily available, children tend to accept that some magical or unnatural causes are at work, a perception not limited to children. As Eugene Subbotsky[35] has pointed out in many of his studies, there are distinct differences between verbally articulating a position and acting on it. In a study that presumed to illustrate that aging in an object can be reversed by immersing the object in a sugary solution, 4- to 6-year-old children refused to drink this "magic" water even when offered a reward out of fear that they might shrink and become younger, despite having earlier asserted that time goes only forward and not backward, that older people can't be made young again. Adults who cherish a photograph of a treasured person will try to protect the picture and slashing it would cause alarm, an experience of causing harm to the individual.

Thus, alongside a more technical understanding of our everyday world we harbor more primitive thoughts and feelings which, for some, involve a world of supernatural forces or spirits and for others a pantheistic feeling that animates all of nature. Surely, the child's conception of magic implies an imagination that is open to possibilities, and his magical thinking, as yet unlike that of an adult, may evolve with time and development into complex constructions that are culturally sanctioned.

Concluding comments

In this chapter we explored the child's emerging capacity to engage in fantasy, to create an imaginary world of emotionally charged thoughts and images, with dreams—the involuntary nightly adventures that suspend time and space—dominated by visual images and words that play a subsidiary role in the drama of the dream world. The fantasy that motivates the daydream is, like the dream, a private affair accessible only to the dreamer who projects, in both images and words, a more pleasing role for the self and its relationships. Moving from the private world to one shared with an audience, thoughts expressed verbally, in the form of made-up stories, soon gain control over the organization of imagined events by arranging them in a temporally and causally ordered sequence that can best convey their meaning. The compositional rule that a story ought to comprise a beginning, a middle, and an end also underpins the fanciful world of the fairytale which, while it presents the listener with an ordered universe, suspends the natural laws of gravity, the finality of gender, of physical appearance, existence, and mortality, and encourages dreams about what is possible, impossible, or improbable and open-ended. Extending our inquiry of fantasy beyond the world of the fairytale which can be seen as circumscribed, a somewhat restricted child-like domain of unreal stories, we discover that magical thinking is not restricted to the childhood years, that magical reasoning is a socially accepted and in part culturally supported manner in which to experience a world that extends beyond the technical cause and effect relations of our daily lives, and may become an avenue for creative inventions in the fields of art as well as science. It is in these different domains of the imagination that children extend their creative endeavors and come to know some of the less manifest aspects of their mental and emotional life.

4

Epilogue

I began this story of imaginative development with children's love of and fascination with art making, their invention of a graphic language and the discoveries they make as they create a visual world composed of forms and colors that can represent their thoughts and feelings. The urge to create alternative worlds, to represent the world as it is or might be, to tell a story, to invent characters and control their fate cuts across all the domains we explored, and it is in the realm of child art that we can follow this evolution in distinct and tangible ways.

When young children make their first efforts to draw and paint, they do not have a readily available model on which to base their drawings and, unlike language with its highly developed symbol system, representing an aspect of their world in drawing requires inventing a language that is not based on simple imitation and copying. Using pencils, markers, and brushes, the intrinsic restrictions of the two-dimensional medium of paper make it literally impossible to "copy" even a simple solid object. The constraints imposed on this medium are even more striking in the case of a human or an animal whose representation is a far cry from the organic nature of the object. Drawing lines, creating simple forms that can stand for the object, and represent it in some fundamental way, is an amazing cultural invention children make as they try to extend this language in personally meaningful ways. Art making, even in childhood, is an act of transformation, of creating a universe on a formerly blank page, an imaginative act of making meaning and coming to understand the object and the self in new ways. The beginning artist is free to experiment, to omit parts, exaggerate others, to annul, to caricature, and engage in a form of dialogue with his or her drawing. Above and beyond the intention to represent is the aesthetic pleasure children feel about their work, the desire to embellish, to decorate, to use color to enhance the emotional appeal of a drawing or painting independent of its reality status.

The imaginative transformation which the child creates on paper is the more remarkable if we consider that the aesthetic impulse predates humans as seen in the eagerness with which chimpanzees and other primates raised in captivity take to painting. Their work is reminiscent of young 2-year-olds and does not progress to a level of representation where forms evoke an image of the intended object. In contrast, child art creates a world of its own composed of lines, dots, shapes, and ornamentation. It is a world that can be revised in the next drawing, as the pull to gain greater veridicality fosters discovery of more sophisticated methods that can bring about a better fit between the image and the object. But even the more realistic depictions are acts of transformation and not a mere copy of reality.

Both drawing and make-believe play are representations that bring about an imaginary transformation of objects and events. In drawing and painting the child's action creates a tangible product that captures a moment in time, and continues to exist even after the action is completed. It can be inspected, lauded, criticized, exhibited or forgotten for the time being, but until it is discarded it has a physical existence. In make-believe play the unfolding actions occur in an extended time frame as the playing child's gestures and commentary transform the self, the partner, and the objects in ways that are relevant to the theme. For example, in pouring make-believe tea from a tea set for the guests of an imaginary party, the transformation is in the pretend act of pouring and drinking, in the pretend identity of the players, and in the verbal interactions that may mimic adult conversation. At the heart of make-believe is an *enactment* which embodies conviction, emotion, and a relation to reality as perceived or wished for. Once the game is over, the only traces to be found are held in the memory of the participants, a memory that may have an impact on the child's sense of self. If one compares the two domains, one notes that the units of production and procedures differ: in drawing there are visible traces of an activity that is relatively permanent and not easily revised, while in the dynamics of pretend play words and gestures that leave no physical record can be momentarily corrected.

One of the defining attributes of pretense play is the ability to move easily between real and pretend identities, and it is this mental transformation that heralds an early form of reversible thought operation in which the pretend identity of the players is maintained for the duration of the game, and the original identity reinstated once the pretense episode is terminated. The ease with which even the young child maintains a dual orientation toward pretense and reality is a mark of flexible thought processes, a form of abstract thought that, at this early stage of development, is quite unique to the domain of make-believe play. One might say that for the playing child the model of the real world has not changed, but its interpretation is novel and opens up new avenues for future thought and action.

From the productive creations of art and make-believe play that are enacted in the public domain, we have come to dreams and daydreams that are solely the province of the individual. The transformation of reality is most extreme in dreams and nightmares; they are products of the mind's attempts to cope with involuntary mental experiences, to scrutinize them and derive insight into the self. To the extent that they are remembered by the adult, the arrow points inward, to the inner world of images, wishes, fears, and failures, but also to the hopes of the dreamer. In the case of children who are the subject of this book, they struggle to understand where the dreams come from and tend to emphasize a connection to everyday experiences and concerns. It is not likely that the remembered dreams hold much significance for their everyday existence other than having some intuitive link with the world of magic and the realm of the fairytale. In the case of nightmares, which are so frequent between ages 3 and 6, children may fear bedtime and going to sleep, and as adults most remember the anxiety-provoking dreams of their childhood which reflected the uncertainties, fears of aggression and of harm experienced by their younger self.

Although daydreams are spun in the personal sphere, we have gained some insight into the role they play in the life of the somewhat older, school-age children who have a fairly clear understanding that they themselves are the producers of these images and scenarios. In many ways the daydreams of these children seem to be a natural extension of their earlier make-believe play to a realm where fantasies are enacted purely in the mind's eye. The ability to conjure up an imaginary world that is compliant and ego-enhancing is a great consolation, and may hold out the promise that it can serve as a potential stage for acting in the real social world. In individuals with a literary inclination daydreams may serve as an early forum for the development of a script, eventually to be written down, or as an avenue for science-related images that facilitate productive thinking in this realm.

Images occupy a central position in drawing, dreams, and daydreams while language, in the form of conversation or commentary, tends to play a subordinate role. It is in the realm of narrative and its many forms that language rules supreme as seen in the nighttime soliloquies of toddlers, the verse stories of preschoolers, and the made-up stories and fairytales of the older children. From an early age the reach of narrative language is extensive and fulfills a central role in the child's life, whether in reviewing the day's events of wishes and prohibitions, worries and consolation or listening to stories that conjure up new worlds of encounters with powerful figures, extraordinary adventures and mishaps.

The stories one constructs for the private self can be loosely organized, but unlike the dream and the daydream, the telling of stories calls for an audience; it is a social event that forges a link between the teller and the listener and needs to be framed in a way that communicates meaning. Unlike the magician, the story teller cannot rely on the performance of magical tricks or on the physical props of make-believe action to capture the audience's attention, and it is purely in the realm of the narrative that his or her skillful use of language and speech evokes meaning, emotions, and the visualization of a scene. This calls for a presentation that adheres to basic rules of time and place, of cause and effect, of moving events from the original setting to a major disruption and effective action that ends in a restoration of the desired state of affairs. As we have seen, tales have to synchronize two parallel worlds: of everyday reality and its pragmatic rules of common sense and causal reasoning, and the inner world of fantasy. From this perspective, magic and magical beliefs are an extended form of narrative that enliven an impersonal universe and humanize it for children and, even more so, for adults who take part in many rituals based on communal beliefs. Story telling is an ancient oral tradition and early exposure to stories fosters an understanding of its basic grammar and a love for the reading of fiction.

The power of representation, the ability to sustain the duality that underpins the relationship between imagination and reality is the common link that unites the domains we have reviewed. These different forms of fantasy fulfill a vital function for the growing child's social, emotional, and cognitive development and hold out the promise for continued innovation and creative engagement.

Notes

1. The Evolution of Child Art

1.   Willats, J. (2005) *Making Sense of Children's Drawings.* Mahwah, NJ: Lawrence Erlbaum Associates.

2.   Gering, V. (1998) The Children's Studio. In C. Golomb (ed.) *The Pavilion of Painting.* Haifa: Ach Publishers, p.90.

3.   Golomb, C. (2004) *The Child's Creation of a Pictorial World,* 2nd ed. Mahwah, NJ: Lawrence Erlbaum Associates.

4.   Selfe, L. (1977) *Nadia: A Case of Extraordinary Drawing Ability in an Autistic Child.* London: Academic Press.

5.   Hermelin, B. (2001) *Bright Splinters of the Mind.* London: Jessica Kingsley Publishers.

6.   Golomb, C. (ed.) (1995) *The Development of Artistically Gifted Children: Selected Case Studies.* Hillsdale, NJ: Lawrence Erlbaum Associates.

7.   Winner, E. (1996) *Gifted Children.* New York, NY: Basic Books.

8.   Interviews conducted two years later reveal that Antonia has been accepted by a prestigious art school as a full time student, on a full scholarship, and that Max has been accepted in a highly competitive summer program of a well known art school, and that he is the recipient of a full scholarship.

9.   Fineberg, J. (1997) *The Innocent Eye.* Princeton, NJ: Princeton University Press.

2. Play: A Wellspring of the Imagination

10. Piaget, J. (1962) *Play, Dreams and Imitation in Childhood*. New York, NY: W. W. Norton & Co.

11. Singer, D. G. and Singer, J. L. (1990) *The House of Make-Believe*. Cambridge, MA: Harvard University Press.

12. Taylor, M. (1999) *Imaginary Companions and the Children Who Create Them*. New York, NY: Oxford University Press.

13. Piaget, J. and Inhelder, B. (1969) *The Psychology of the Child*. New York, NY: Basic Books.

14. Paley, V. (1981) *Wally's Stories*. Cambridge, MA: Harvard University Press.

15. Axline, V. (1964) *Dibs in Search of Self*. Boston, MA: Houghton Mifflin Co.

3. Between Fantasy and Fiction

16. Foulkes, D. (1999) *Childrens' Dreaming and the Development of Consciousness*. Cambridge, MA: Harvard University Press.

17. Piaget, J. (1962) *Play, Dreams, and Imitation*. New York, NY: W. W. Norton & Company.

18. Singer, J. (1976) *The Inner World of Daydreaming*. New York, NY: Harper & Row.

19. Rosenfeld, E., Huesmann, L. R., Eron, L. D., and Torney-Purta, J. V. (1982) Measuring patterns of fantasy behavior in children. *Journal of Personality and Social Psychology*, 42 (2), pp.347–366.

20. Strauch, I. and Lederbogen, S. (1999) The home dreams and waking fantasies of boys and girls between ages 9 and 15: A longitudinal study. *Dreaming*, 9 (2/3), pp.153–161.

21. Lord, A. B. (1960) *The Singer of Tales*. Cambridge, MA: Harvard University Press.

22. Leondar, B. (1977) Hatching plots: Genesis of story making. In D. Perkins and B. Leondar (eds) *The Arts and Cognition*. Baltimore, MD: The John Hopkins Press.

23. Maranda, E. K. and Maranda, P. (1971) *Structural Models in Folklore and Transformational Essays*. The Hague: Mouton.

24. Weir, R. H. (1970) *Language in the Crib*. The Hague: Mouton.

25. Nelson, K. (1989) (ed.) *Narratives from the Crib*. Cambridge, MA: Harvard University Press.

26. Pitcher, E. G. and Prelinger, E. (1963) *Children Tell Stories: An Analysis of Fantasy*. New York, NY: International Universities Press.

27. Sutton-Smith, B. (1981) *The Folk Stories of Children*. Philadelphia, PA: The University of Pennsylvania Press.

28. Chukovsky, K. (1971) *From Two to Five*. Berkeley, CA: University of California Press.

29. Bettelheim, B. (1975) *The Uses of Enchantment*. New York, NY: Vintage Books.

30. Crain, W. C., D'Alessio, E., McIntyre, B., and Smoke, L. (1983) The impact of hearing a fairytale on children's immediate behavior. *The Journal of Genetic Psychology*, 143, pp.9–17.

31. Coulacoglou, C. (ed.) (2008) *Exploring the Child's Personality*. Springfield, IL: Charles C. Thomas Publishers.

32. Woolley, J. D. and Cox, V. (2007) Development of beliefs about storybook reality. *Developmental Science*, 10 (5), pp.681–693.

33. Piaget, J. (1929) *The Child's Conception of the World*. London: Kegan Paul.

34. Roengren, K. S., Johnson, C. N., and Harris, P. L. (eds) (2000) *Imagining the Impossible*. New York, NY: Cambridge University Press.

35. Subbotsky, E. (1994) Early rationality and magical thinking in preschoolers: Space and time. *British Journal of Developmental Psychology*, 12, pp.97–108.

Further Reading

Arnheim, R. (1974) *Art and Visual Perception*. Berkeley, CA: University of California Press.

Aronson, J. and Golomb, C. (1999) Preschoolers' understanding of pretense and presumption of congruence between action and representation. *Developmental Psychology*, 35 (6), pp.1414–1425.

Bretherton, I. (ed.) (1984) *Symbolic Play: The Development of Social Understanding*. New York, NY: Academic Press.

Briggs, J. L. (1998) *Inuit Morality Play*. New Haven, CT: Yale University Press.

Cashdan, S. (1999) *The Witch Must Die*. New York, NY: Basic Books.

Clark, G. and Zimmerman, E. (2004) *Teaching Talented Art Students: Principles and Practice*. New York: Teachers College Press and Reston, VA: National Art Education Association.

Cohen, D. and Mackeith, S. (1991) *The Development of Imagination*. New York, NY: Routledge.

Coulacoglou, C. (ed.) (2008) *Exploring the Child's Personality*. Springfield, IL: Charles C. Thomas Publishers.

Cox, M. (1992) *Children's Drawings*. London: Penguin Books.

Dement, W. and Kleitman, N. (1957) The relation of eye movements during sleep to dream activity: An objective method for the study of dreaming. *Journal of Experimental Psychology*, 53, pp.339–346.

Domhoff, G. W. (1996) *Finding Meaning in Dreams*. New York, NY: Plenum Press.

Garfield, P. L. (1984) *Your Child Dreams*. New York, NY: Ballantine.

Golomb, C. (1977) The role of substitutions in pretense and puzzle games. *The British Journal of Educational Psychology*, 47, pp.175–186.

Golomb, C. (guest ed.) (1996) Drawing development and artistry in mentally handicapped persons. Special issue, *Visual Arts Research*, 22 (2).

Golomb, C. and Barr-Grossman, T. (1977) Representational development of the human figure in the familial retardate. *Genetic Psychology Monographs*, 95, pp.247–266.

Golomb, C. and Cornelius, C. (1977) Symbolic play and its cognitive significance. *Developmental Psychology*, 13, pp.246–252.

Golomb, C. and Galasso, L. (1995) Make-believe and reality: Explorations of the imaginary realm. *Developmental Psychology*, 40 (5), pp.800–810.

Golomb, C., Goranson Gowing, E. and Friedman, L. (1982) Play and cognition: Studies in pretense play and conservation of quantity. *Journal of Experimental Psychology*, 33, pp.257–279.

Golomb, C. and Kuersten, R. (1996) On the transition from pretense play to reality: What are the rules of the game? *British Journal of Developmental Psychology*, 14, pp. 203–217.

Göncü, A. and Gaskins, S. (2007) *Play and Development.* Mahwah, NJ: Lawrence Erlbaum Associates.

Hartman, E. (2001) *Dream and Nightmares: The New Theory of the Origin and Meaning of Dreams.* New York, NY: Basic Books.

Klinger, E. (1990) *Daydreams.* Los Angeles, CA: Jeremy Tarcher.

Laurendeau, M. and Pinard, A. (1962) *Causal Thinking in the Child.* New York, NY: International Universities Press.

Matthews, J. (1999) *The Art of Childhood and Adolescence.* London: Palmer Press.

Milbrath, C. (1998) *Patterns of Artistic Development in Children.* New York, NY: Cambridge University Press.

Nicolopoulou, A. (1997) Children and narratives: Toward an interpretive and sociocultural approach. In M. Bamberg (ed.) *Narrative Development: Six Approaches*, pp.175–215. Mahwah, NJ: Lawrence Erlbaum Associates.

Paley, V. (1984) *Boys and Girls. Superheroes in the Doll Corner.* Chicago, IL: University of Chicago Press.

Paley, V. (1990) *The Boy Who Would be a Helicopter.* Cambridge, MA: Harvard University Press.

Phelps, K. E. and Woolley, J. D. (1994) The form and function of young children's magical beliefs. *Developmental Psychology*, 30, pp.385–394.

Prince, C. (1973) *A Grammar of Stories.* The Hague: Mouton.

Propp, V. (1968) *The Morphology of the Folktale.* Austin, TX: University of Texas Press.

Scarlett, G. and Wolf, D. (1979) When it's only make-believe: The construction of a boundary between fantasy and reality in story telling. *New Directions for Child Development*, 6, pp.29–40.

Stern, N. (1988) The development of children's story telling skill. In M. B. Franklin and S. Barten (eds) *Child Language: A Reader*, pp.282–297. New York, NY: Oxford University Press.

Subbotsky, E. V. (1993) *Foundations of the Mind.* Cambridge, MA: Harvard University Press.

Warner, M. (1995) *From the Beast to the Blond.* New York, NY: Farrar Strauss.

Woolley, J. D. (1995) The fictional mind: Young children's understanding of imagination, pretense, and dreams. *Developmental Review*, 15, pp.172–211.

Woolley, J. D. and Boerger, E. A. (2002) Development of beliefs about the origins and controllability of dreams. *Developmental Psychology*, 38 (1), pp.24–41.

Index